Modern
Magickal Keys

Modern Magickal Keys

A Contemporary Grimoire
for Personal Transformation

THOMAS EISELE

ABRAMELIN PRESS

New York, New York

Abramelin Press
c/o Thomas Eisele
P.O. Box 640
Inwood Post Office
New York, New York 10034-0640

Copyright 2004 by Thomas Eisele
Copyright all Illustrations and Graphics 2004 by Thomas Eisele
Layout & Design: David Greenbaum

ISBN 0-9753191-0-8

Printed in the United States of America

*This book is dedicated
to the memory of
my dearest friend,*

Rosa Alcántara.

ACKNOWLEDGEMENTS

I would like to begin by thanking the New York Chapter
of The Association for Research and Enlightenment (A.R.E.) for
providing me with numerous opportunities to present my work.

I would also like to thank John Savarese, Gertrude, and Aldee Filley
for their vision and commitment to publishing this book.

Finally, with the deepest appreciation, I wish to acknowledge Tifani,
Daniel, and Hector Peguero for their kindness and support.

Table of Contents

INTRODUCTION

When I began my path as a spiritual teacher, I quickly became aware of the inherent problem that exists in attempting to instruct people on how to develop their Psychic or Intuitive abilities. The basic nature of this problem is rooted in the fact that a quantum leap of faith is being asked of people when they are simply not equipped with a sufficient enough understanding of the Universe to make such a jump possible. The reason for this inherent limitation is because education in the society at large is mainly about standardization and conformity, the intention being to maintain the existing social structure by influencing the perspectives of its members. That our social system and its values are for the most part arbitrary is obscured by a fear of material failure which permeates the mentality of most people. The euphemistic box that has been placed over our perceptions from childhood is what we understand as "reality," which thereby reduces much of what is outside the box to either fear or illusion. The great psychologist and visionary Wilhelm Reich called this phenomenon of control "The Emotional Plague," a gruesomely poetic yet apt description for the thwarting of the natural, creative development of the individual.

After encountering many of the aforementioned blockages in the vast majority of people, I feel it is a testament to the power of the natural Spiritual Forces within humanity that despite the behavior modification exercised by the society at large, there are still many individuals who are nonetheless responding to their intuitive urges and looking toward an alternative Spirituality. On one level this is good in that many are now trying to go beyond what has been limiting their perceptions, but on another level a new problem has emerged because most of these individuals, though well intentioned, are still at a loss as to how they can actually live beyond the standards of the box. Even though the erroneous logic that they have been taught is essentially an illusion, most people still need to hold onto something of that tradition when they initially attempt to experience the Universe beyond the confines of conventional reality.

The Ancient Magicians referred to the journey of attempting to go beyond the apparent limitations of material reality as "Initiation" and subsequently established "Mystery Schools" to provide training for those who sought to embrace the Universe beyond the 5 human senses. The theory guiding this training was simple enough; to provide a basic language by which a new understanding of the world could be explored. A more mundane example of this would be if a person was suddenly uprooted from their home in Brooklyn and transported to a small town in France. With no knowledge of the language or customs in this new place, chances are this individual would have a very tough time getting around. However, if this person had been prepared in advance with a year of instruction on how to speak French they would probably be better able to make a successful adjustment to their new environment. With the preceding in mind, what I have attempted to do in this book is to present a system through which the reader can expand their notion of "reality" by utilizing the symbolic languages of Western Mysticism. Once these fundamentals are in place, the book then offers original examples of how this new grammar can be used to create tools by which to begin fashioning a new way of thinking and being beyond the "box" of conventional reality. It is not the intention of this work to establish a new set of rules about what reality is, rather it is a manual to be initially read through once and then consulted when necessary as the student applies the principles included to the unique circumstances of their own life.

In describing his legendary periodical of the Spiritual Arts known as "The Equinox" Aleister Crowley wrote "The Aim of Religion, the Method of Science." In an attempt to follow a similar grounded approach, I now present "Modern Magickal Keys."

PART I

MAGICKAL LANGUAGE

CHAPTER I

MAGICK

HEN people hear the term, "Magic," they tend to think of the modern stereotype of a man in a tuxedo pulling a rabbit out of a hat, yet that is nothing more than trickery or sleight of hand. High Magick (with a "k") that incorporates ritual along with sacred symbolism is about pulling God forth from within one's self, not fooling around with rabbits or hats.

Probably the most succinct definition of Higher Magick was coined by Aleister Crowley (1875-1947), arguably the premier Mage of the 20th Century, when he declared Magick to be "The Science and Art of causing change to occur in conformity with Will." On its most basic level that is all Magick really is, transforming intention into manifestation, although the key word in Crowley's definition is "Will" which should not be confused with the lower vibrational phenomena of either ego or desire. To differentiate between the lower aspects of Will and its Higher manifestation, Crowley developed a concept he called the "True Will." In "The Book of the Law" Crowley writes, "For pure will, unassuaged of purpose, delivered from the lust of result, is every way perfect." For Crowley, the Magickal Will represented the conscious discovery and development of the purpose of the self in relation to the universe. In "Magick in Theory and Practice" he also writes, "Every man has a right to fulfill his own will without being afraid that it may interfere with that of others; for if he is in his proper place, it is the fault of others if they interfere with him."

Crowley believed the most efficient way to apprehend one's True Will was through the use of Ritual Magick, a codified system of actions and symbols designed to awaken the dormant Higher Consciousness within each individual. Once this power is ignited, then the flame of enlightenment can be kindled and a greater perspective on life and its relative meaning can be attained.

The actual practice of Ritual Magick is about Healing through self-empowerment. The practitioner attains this by intentionally activating certain archetypal energies within the self through the utilization of outward symbols associated with these same archetypes. For example, if I ceremonially invoke the energies of the Goddess Venus through the saying of certain words and the performance of certain predetermined actions, I am really in effect summoning those same aspects of the Goddess that already exist within me so that I may subsequently attract the reflections of this inner energy from the outer world. On even the most mundane level this approach makes perfect sense, for how could I ever hope for love or beauty to manifest in my life if these things did not first exist within me?

For the most part, the practice of Ritual Magick has always been largely misunderstood by the general public. This is because Magick has been disowned and demonized throughout the ages. The inner awakening which is the purpose of Magick is the ultimate expression of individual freedom.

So far, this chapter on Magick has only focused on the general theoretical aspects of the Art. Supposing that whoever might be reading this has had their interest aroused, what are the specifics for the practice of Ritual Magick? In the following chapters the reader will learn about the 3 branches that constitute the language of Magick (Qabalah, Astrology, and Tarot) along with how this language can be used with Sacred Shapes to construct a "talisman" or a picture of our intentions for transformation. Once this talisman has been made, the final step will be to empower or "electrify" it with Spirit through the use of Ritual. This construction and consecration of a Magickal Key or "talisman" will then essentially represent an encapsulation of what practicing Magicians refer to as, "The Great Work," which is the conscious attempt to unify Above (the Higher Self or the True Will) and Below (manifest physical reality) within the Magician so that he or she has a perfect awareness of who they are in the Universe as it evolves.

Many years ago, a writer by the name of Aldous Huxley wrote a pioneering book entitled, "The Doors of Perception." The next 14 chapters of this present volume should be looked upon as a ring of keys, Magickal Keys, to unlock these doors to which Huxley was referring.

❖❖❖

CHAPTER II

THE QABALAH

HEN one endeavors to embark upon the path of the Initiate and commence a study of Western Ritual Magick the basic concepts to be mastered are those that exist in the Holy Qabalah of the Hebrews. Essentially a methodology for revealing the underlying Mystical interpretation of Hebrew Scripture, the Qabalah provides a system of symbolism that furnishes the Magician with the parameters through which he or she may understand and gauge their individual experience. The basic diagram into which this system is organized is the "Tree of Life," a structure composed of 10 spheres (or vortices of energy) connected by 22 pathways that together constitute the Spiritual or "Heavenly Body" within each individual human being. Each of the spheres on the Tree of Life are then subsequently intended to represent an archetypal aspect of what it means to be a complete being formulated as an extension of the One Unified Will of the Universe.

In this discussion I will place these Spheres at their various locations on the physical body and the reader will no doubt notice that this placing is the opposite of the way the Spheres appear in the furnished diagram. It should be kept in mind that the diagram as it appears on the printed page is a mirror image and needs to be reversed. For example, if one were to look at an Anatomy textbook the heart would be on the right side of a full body or torso illustration from the viewpoint of looking at the book, however, it is common knowledge that the heart is located on the left side of the chest. Beyond this basic logic, I also feel it is necessary to reverse the printed Tree when applying it to the body because the Tree of Life represents the heavenly prototype of existence, or God, and by not reversing the diagram one is effectively saying that God is something other from all of us as individual human beings. It was mentioned earlier that through his or her work a Magician endeavors to pull God out from within the self much like the Illusionists attempt to pull rabbits out of hats. If that is the case then it is important to embrace this inner Divine essence with conscious intent if one hopes to be at all successful.

The 10 Spheres of the Tree of Life are initially divided into four groups otherwise known as "The Four Worlds." The first of these is known as Olam Atziluth or "The World of Archetypes" and consists of the first Sphere that is called, "Kether" (Crown). The second group includes the second and third spheres of "Chokmah" (Wisdom) and "Binah" (Understanding) and is referred to as Olam Briah or "The World of Creation." The third group is called Olam Yetzirah or "The World of Formation" and includes in order the fourth through the ninth spheres of "Chesed" (Mercy), "Geburah" (Might), "Tiphareth" (Beauty), "Netzach" (Victory), "Hod" (Splendor), and "Yesod" (Foundation). The remaining tenth sphere known as "Malkuth" (Kingdom), constitutes Olam Assiah or "The World of Action."

At this point, we are now ready to briefly look at the archetypal symbolism of the 10 Sephiroth or "Spheres" that form the Tree of Life as well as how these various vortices relate to the 4 Worlds.

THE TREE OF LIFE

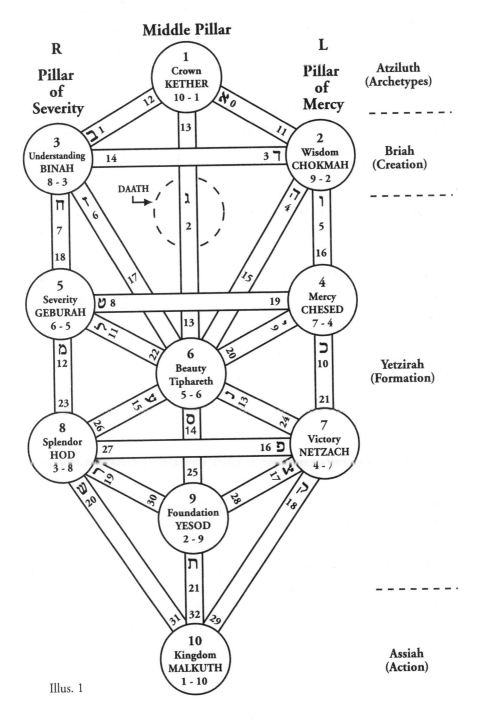

Illus. 1

KETHER

Located at the top of the head where it forms the World of Archetypes or "Olam Atziluth" is the first sphere of Kether which is translated from the Hebrew as "Crown." Kether represents the dimensionless point where the Divine, limitless light known as "Ain Soph Aur" enters into each individual. This is the point on the Tree where the life force is in the pure state of an androgynous energy as yet untainted by the duality of our earthly existence. Kether can be viewed as the processing point where our Higher Selves must leave their Divine attire at the door to don work clothes for the challenges and lessons of this earthly dimension. The planetary influence which rules over Kether is that of the Galactic Center, that greater central point beyond our Solar System that represents higher dimensions of consciousness. The oldest recognized Qabalistic text known as The Sepher Yetzirah or "Book of Formation" refers to Kether as the "Admirable" or "Hidden Intelligence." Its color is white and its element is the diamond.

CHOKMAH

Located on the left side of the head, approximately behind the left ear, is the second sephirah known as Chokmah or "Wisdom" which is the first of the two spheres comprising Olam Briah or "The World of Creation." This sphere represents the first element of duality and serves as the initial process that the intellect enacts upon the Divine, androgynous light received from Kether. Chokmah is also known as "The First Potentiator" for it contains the vital energy necessary to initiate existence, an energy that the Chinese Taoists refer to as the "Yang Force." Psychologically, this sphere corresponds to the left side of the brain which is linear, logical, and male. The ruling planetary influence over Chokmah is that of Uranus, the archetype of revolutionary change and unbridled creativity. In the Sepher Yetzirah Chokmah is known as "The Illuminating Intelligence."

BINAH

The other sphere included in The World of Creation or "Olam Briah" is located on the right side of the head, approximately behind the right ear, and represents the third Sephirah known as Binah or "Understanding." Binah is considered the basic female archetype and is associated with the mother and the potential that exists within the darkness of the Great Void. It represents the other half of the duality initiated by Chokmah and would correspond in Taoism as Yin to Chokmah's Yang. I feel the translation of "Understanding" from the Hebrew is particularly apt in that understanding implies the ability to absorb within one the essence of something and this receptive ability is a quintessentially feminine trait. Psychologically, Binah is associated with the right brain which is creative, intuitive, and female. The ruling planetary influence is that of Saturn, the archetype of divine, natural structure, and in the Sepher Yetzirah Binah is referred to as "The Sanctifying Intelligence."

The first three Spheres that have just been written about are also known as "The Supernals" and depict the idea of a pure, unified consciousness that splits into the basic duality of male and female.

Following Binah on the descent down the Tree of Life is an 11th Sphere that is not considered a Sephirah in the formal sense. Known as Daath or "Knowledge" in Hebrew and located over the throat, this vortex is also sometimes referred to as "The Abyss" in that it represents the totality of all knowledge which would therefore also include the unknown. Ruled by Pluto, the planetary archetype of change and transformation, Daath is the realm of our lessons and the obstacles we will encounter along the journey of our evolution during this lifetime.

Below Daath, the next 6 Spheres constitute The World of Formation or "Olam Yetzirah" and represent the various levels and dimensions of Earthly duality.

Before continuing with this outline of the 10 Sephiroth, I would like to pause briefly to discuss how the Tree of Life is also divided vertically into 3 pillars and how the designations of male and female are applied to the various Spheres below Daath.

In considering the diagram of the Tree of Life, all of the Spheres on the left side (when the Tree is applied to the body) which include Chokmah, Chesed, and Netzach are referred to as "The Pillar of Mercy." All of the Spheres on the right side which include Binah, Geburah, and Hod are known as "The Pillar of Severity." The remaining four Spheres that extend down the center of the Tree, Kether, Tiphareth, Yesod, and Malkuth are called "The Middle Pillar" (refer back to diagram). Where matters get a little tricky is that the Spheres contained in the Pillar of Mercy are considered male, yet below Chokmah these Spheres are given female attributes. The Spheres included in the Pillar of Severity are considered female, yet below Binah these Spheres are given male attributes. To my mind, this mingling of gender speaks to both the profundity and universality of the Qabalistic mindset in that the Ancient Hebrew Adepts recognized the duality or "Yin-Yang" quality of Earthly existence just as the Taoist's did. Each human being holds the essence of both sexes within their being regardless which sort of genitalia they may be equipped with. For example, if a man hopes to attain his highest Spiritual potential he must be able to embrace his abilities to receive and nurture, both of which are feminine qualities. Also the fact that the male and female aspects of Chokmah and Binah, located in the left and right brain respectively, end up crossing over their influences below the Abyss to the opposite side of the body coincides perfectly with the Modern Physiological axiom of the left brain controlling the right side of the body and the right brain controlling the left side of the body.

To eliminate the above material from being confusing, the approach I have subsequently developed is to consider the gender of the Spheres based solely on their individual attributes. As a result, from here on I will speak of the Spheres in the Pillar of Mercy below Chokmah as female, and the Spheres in the Pillar of Severity below Binah as male. The remaining Spheres that comprise the Middle Pillar are considered androgynous in that they represent a mediation between the polarities of male and female.

CHESED

Located at the left shoulder is the fourth Sphere of Chesed, also known as "Gedulah," both of which translate from the Hebrew as meaning "Mercy." Chesed is the first Sphere of the World of Formation (Olam Yetzirah) and can be viewed in terms of an individual's Yin expansion or the ability to receive and embrace life in an unconditionally loving and non-judgmental way. The planetary ruler of Chesed is Jupiter, the archetype of benevolence, beneficence, and expansiveness. Referred to in the ancient text of the Sepher Yetzirah as "The Receptacular Intelligence" the sacred animals of Chesed are the Horse and its mythical brother the Unicorn.

GEBURAH

The fifth Sphere is located at the right shoulder and is known as Geburah or "Severity." Representing the second sphere in the World of Formation, the ruling planetary influence of this sphere is Mars, the God of War from Roman Mythology. As an archetype, Mars represents the raw strength or force necessary to manifest results, though not necessarily the judgment or discernment to manifest our desires in a balanced way. As opposed to Chesed, Geburah stands for the Yang expansion of the individual or the way we seek our desires in the world. In the Norse pantheon, the God of Thunder or "Thor" is attributed to this path as he also doubled as the God of War in that belief system. The color associated with Geburah is red and its title in the Sepher Yetzirah is "The Radical Intelligence."

TIPHARETH

The sixth Sphere is named Tiphareth or "Beauty" and would correspond to the Heart Chakra of Hindu Mysticism. Tiphareth is the third of the six Spheres in the World of Formation and is located at the geographical center of both the physical body and the Tree of Life where it serves as a balancing centrifugal influence for the other Spheres. Because of its central location, the ruling planetary influence of Tiphareth is the Sun and the Sphere represents the loving ideal of harmony and balance between the constantly shifting polarities of the male and female energies expressed in the four surrounding Spheres on the right and left pillars. The Sepher Yetzirah names Tiphareth "The Mediating Intelligence" and the animal attributions for this Sphere are the Phoenix, that legendary bird of resurrection, and the Lion.

NETZACH

The seventh Sphere is known as "Netzach" and its translation from the Hebrew is, "Victory." Netzach is the fourth of the six Spheres in the World of Formation and is located on the body at the left hip. The symbolism associated with this Sphere is that of sexual love and the harvest. The energy of Netzach is decidedly female and its ruling planetary influence is that of Venus, the Divine archetype of love and the regenerative forces of nature. This Sphere is also associated with our artistic urges which are essentially a metaphor for the reproductive act in that the creation of a work of Art involves the implanting of an impression that subsequently requires a gestation period before a recreation of our understanding can be presented to the world. The Egyptian Goddess Hathor, the Cow Goddess, is also attributed to this path for to the peoples of Ancient Egypt this archetype symbolized the regenerative power of nature as expressed through the fruits of the Earth. The Sphere of Netzach also holds influence over our intuitions and in the Sepher Yetzirah this vortex is referred to as "The Occult Intelligence." Its sacred flower is the rose and its sacred stone is the emerald.

HOD

Located on the right hip, the eighth Sphere is known as "Hod" and its translation from Hebrew is, "Splendor." On a lower plane, Hod represents many of the same qualities as Chokmah for it is the male potentiality in the gross physical realm as opposed to the pure male archetype of the Supernals. The ruling planetary influence over this Sphere is Mercury and the power in this vortex resides with the mental body. In Greek Mythology, Mercury was the Divine Messenger of the Gods and could gain access to any plane of existence. He is credited as being the divine author of such systems of knowledge as Language, Mathematics, Alchemy, and Tarot. Thoth, the Egyptian equivalent of Mercury, is also attributed to this Sphere. The Sepher Yetzirah refers to Hod as "The Absolute or Perfect Intelligence" and it represents the fifth of the six Spheres included in the World of Formation.

YESOD

The last of the Spheres constituting the World of Formation is the ninth Sephirah which is named "Yesod" and whose translation from Hebrew into English is "Foundation." Located at the genital area of the body, Yesod symbolizes the point where the polarities of energy below the Abyss rejoin in order to make a grounding connection with the Mother Earth. According to Madame Blavatsky, the renowned author and founder of the Theosophical Society, Yesod represents the Astral Plane, the subtle, all permeating matter that provides the foundation for our physical reality. The ruling planetary energy of Yesod is the Moon, which signifies not only the subconscious but also Mysticism and Psychic abilities. The ability to trust in our power as co-creators of the life we are manifesting also resides in this Sphere. In the Sepher Yetzirah the name for Yesod is, "The Pure or Clear Intelligence." Its plant is Damiana, a known aphrodisiac, and its color is purple.

MALKUTH

The last of the four Worlds that make up the Tree of Life, namely Olam Assiah or "The World of Action" is comprised entirely of the tenth Sphere of Malkuth which translates from the Hebrew as "Kingdom." This is the Sphere that represents the physical world of matter and includes the four elements of Occult Philosophy (air, fire, earth, and water) as well as all the forms capable of being perceived by our five senses. Aptly enough, the ruling planetary Sphere of Malkuth is the Earth. The Sphere of Malkuth also represents a synthesis for the ideas and concepts exemplified by the preceding nine Spheres for it provides the environment in which these ideas become manifest. From a Magickal standpoint, Malkuth also provides the base to recycle the divine energy coming down from Kether after it has passed back and forth like a lightning bolt through the other Spheres. After this energy has grounded in Malkuth, it will rise again to form a Caduceus of Kundalini-like energy on the way back up to the Crown. This flow of energy up and down the Tree of Life is expressed in the Qabalistic axiom "Kether is in Malkuth and Malkuth is in Kether," a concept that can be mundanely illustrated by folding a diagram of the Tree of Life in half so that the crease divides Tiphareth horizontally into a pair of equal sections. The Sepher Yetzirah refers to Malkuth as "The Resplendent Intelligence" and the mythological attribution to the Sphere is "Ceres," the Greek Goddess of the Earth.

THE PATHWAYS

There are 22 Pathways that connect the 10 Spheres of the Tree of Life. These paths are numbered from 11 to 32 and continue the overall numerical format established by the 10 Spheres. Each of these pathways in turn are attributed a different letter of the Hebrew alphabet (assigned to the paths in order) as well as one of the 22 Trumps of the Major Arcana of the Tarot (also assigned to the paths in order coinciding with the cards respective numbers within the deck). The pairings of the Hebrew alphabet to the Pathways can be viewed in the diagram of the Tree of Life presented at the beginning of this chapter, while the Tarot associations can be seen in the diagram that immediately follows this paragraph. The number cards which constitute the Minor Arcana of the Tarot (Ace to 10) are applied in numerical order to the Spheres, while the Court Cards (King, Queen, Knight, and Page) are applied in descending order beginning with the Kings to the spheres of Chokmah, Binah, Tiphareth, and Malkuth respectively. A second table will follow the one containing the Tarot attributions to the Tree of Life and in that diagram the reader will be shown the Astrological and Elemental attributions to the Tree. From this data, one will then be able to see how the Tree of Life serves as an interlocking superstructure for the three symbolic languages of the Hebrew Alphabet, Tarot, and Astrology.

THE TAROT IN THE TREE OF LIFE

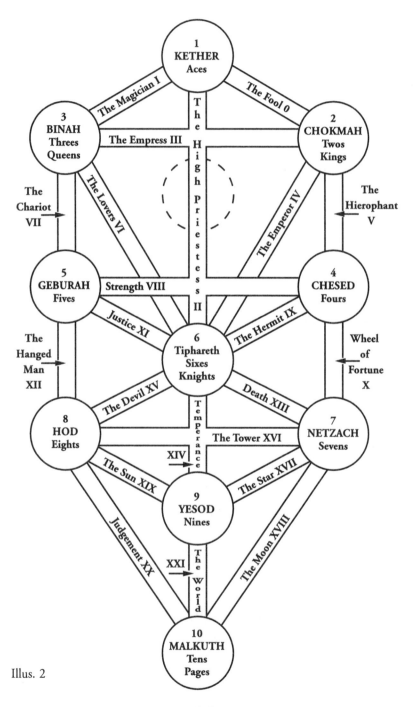

Illus. 2

ASTROLOGY SIGNS AND ELEMENTS
IN THE TREE OF LIFE

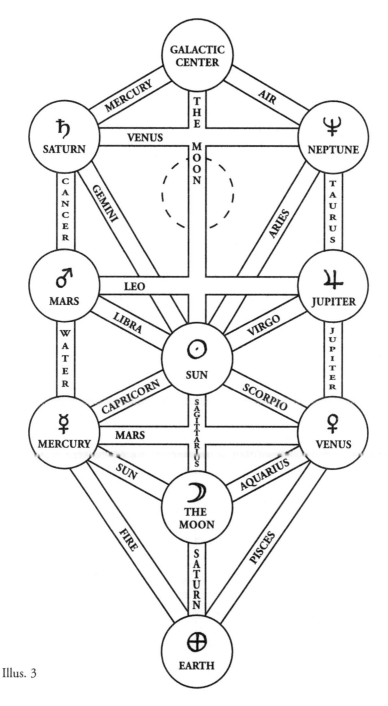

Illus. 3

THE LITERAL QABALAH

Now that the basic concepts of the Tree of Life have been explained, let us next examine what is known as "The Literal Qabalah."

The 22 letters of the Hebrew alphabet that are applied to the Pathways of the Tree of Life also double as numbers, there being no separate number system in Ancient Hebrew as there is in Modern English with our Roman numerals. From this concept of a unified alphabet and number system there developed the Ancient Science of Gematria, whereby words in Hebrew with the same numerical value are considered to be explanatory of each other. Illustration 4 is a table showing the Hebrew alphabet along with the numerical equivalents of the letters and their English translations.

THE HEBREW ALPHABET

Hebrew Letter	Numerical Value	Hebrew Letter Name	Signification of Name	Roman Letter
א	1	Aleph	Ox, also Duke, or Leader	A
ב	2	Beth	House	B
ג	3	Gimel	Camel	G
ד	4	Daleth	Door	D
ה	5	He	Window	H
ו	6	Vau	Peg, Nail	V
ז	7	Zayin	Weapon, Sword	Z
ח	8	Cheth	Enclosure, Fence	Ch
ט	9	Teth	Serpent	T
י	10	Yod	Hand	I
כ Final = ך	20 Final = 500	Kaph	Palm of the hand	K
ל	30	lamed	Ox-Goad	L
מ Final = ם	40 Final = 600	Mem	Water	M
נ Final = ן	50 Final = 700	Nun	Fish	N
ס	60	Samekh	Prop, Support	S
ע	70	Ayin	Eye	O
פ Final = ף	80 Final = 800	Pe	Mouth	P
צ Final = ץ	90 Final = 900	Tzaddi	Fishing-hook	Tz
ק	100	Qoph	Back of the head	Q
ר	200	Resh	Head	R
ש	300	Shin	Tooth	S, Sh
ת	400	Tau	Sign of the Cross	T, Th

Illus. 4

After looking over the preceding information, the reader will undoubtedly notice there are two forms with different numerical values for each of the following five letters; Kaph (K), Mem (M), Nun (N), Peh (P), and Tzaddi (Tz). The second form, which is attributed the higher numerical value, is known as the final form and applies when any of the preceding letters is used as the last letter in a word. It should also be pointed out that in this table of the alphabet the highest numerical value is the final form of the letter Tzaddi at 900. To represent values in the thousands a letter is written larger, for instance, a large Aleph is 1000, a large Beth is 2000, and so on, or a dash can be drawn above the letter.

Now let's work out an example of Gematria using the Hebrew words for Love (AHBH) and Unity (AchD). The numerical breakdown for the first word is, A=1, H=5, B=2, H=5, thus AHBH= 13. In the second word, A=1, Ch=8, D=4, so that AchD also has a numerical total of 13. In this case the connection between the words "Love" and "Unity" is somewhat obvious, however, where the more sublime aspects of Gematria become evident is when words that seemingly possess contradictory meanings turn out to have the same numerical values. For instance, the Hebrew word AIB, which means "Hated," also has a numerical value of 13 (A=1, I=10, and B=2).

In this case, Gematria reveals a trinity between the three words cited whereby a more complete meaning comes into focus for each of them in terms of embracing a higher understanding. Both love and hate, which are usually looked upon as being complete polar opposites, can now be viewed as containing aspects that in some way must be complementary in order for unity to truly have any meaning.

A second example of Gematria that may be of interest to the reader can be seen in a literal translation of my name into Hebrew;

Thomas ="Teth (9), Heh (5), Ayin (70), Mem (40), Aleph (1), Samekh (60)" Eisele = "Heh (5), Yod (10), Samekh (60), Heh (5), Lamed (30), Heh (5)

My first name has a value of 185 when it is translated literally into Hebrew and my last name has a value of 115. The combined total of my full name would therefore be 300, the value of the Hebrew expression RVCh ALHIM or "Ruach Elohim" which literally means "The Breath of Spirit." I have given this example so that the reader will be able to see how a connection to Spirit must often be forged by making a conscious effort at a direct personal connection to the work at hand. By revealing "The Breath of Spirit" within the essence of my name, I was able to find a deeper esoteric reason for my explorations into The Qabalah and thus the inspiration to continue on.

Another element to be noted regarding Hebrew is that it is a language consisting entirely of consonants. To indicate a vowel placement a small symbol known as a "dogesh," represented by a small black dot, is placed below the letter. While causing changes in pronunciation, a dogesh will have no effect whatsoever in Gematria. I only mention this because vowels in English such as A and E can be omitted when transliterating from English into Hebrew if doing so would create a more advantageous Gematric scheme. For example, the name for the first sphere in the Tree of Life is written as "Kether" in English, yet in Hebrew it is spelled "KThR" with the dogesh being placed under the letter Kaph (K). When using Gematria, there are other choices one has when translating back and forth between English and Hebrew. For instance, the Hebrew letters Shin (Sh) and Samekh (S) can be substituted for the English letter "S," although the numerical value for each is quite different with Shin equaling 300 and Samekh equaling 60. As a result, to some extent one may manipulate the numerical value of a word translated from English into Hebrew to gain a more suitable outcome for your intentions. This sort of substitution also works for the letters Teth (T) and Tav (Th) with Teth equaling 9 and Tav equaling 400. This information is important to keep in mind when attempting to find the Gematria of one's name since a literal transposing of every letter into Hebrew might not work well. Needless to say, there are many rules as well as irregularities to be aware of when translating English into Hebrew and vice-versa, but since this is not a textbook on how to speak Hebrew I will not go into the matter any further. I believe that enough information has been provided with the table of the Hebrew alphabet and my subsequent explanations for the reader to be able to fully understand the use of Gematria as it applies to the rest of this book.

Besides Gematria, there are two other systems that provide additional levels of Spiritual meaning to the Hebrew language and they are known as "Notariqon" and "Temurah." As explained by S.L. Mathers in the introduction to his book "The Kabbalah Unveiled," Notariqon is derived from the Latin "Notarius" meaning "a shorthand writer" and is a way of creating acronyms. There are two forms of Notariqon. In the first, every letter of a specific word is utilized as the beginning letter in each of several subsequent words to create a new sentence. The example Mathers gives is the first word in Genesis, Berashith, or in Hebrew, BRAShITh, which can have each of its letters used to create the following sentence; BRAShITh RAH ALHIM ShIQBLV IShRAL ThVRH or "In the beginning God saw that Israel would accept the Law." The second type of Notariqon is the opposite of the first, using the beginning, middle, or final letter of each word in a sentence to form a new word. An example of this would be the word "ARARITA" which is formed by using the first letter of each word in the following sentence; **Achad Raysheethoh**; **Achad Resh Iechidathoh**; **Temurathoh Achad** or "One is his beginning; One is his individuality; his permutation is one."

Temurah is translated as "Permutation" and though there are several forms I will only explain the two most commonly used. The first is called "The Tables of the Combinations of Tziruph" and consists of folding the alphabet in half and then exchanging the letters in the second half so that a series of commutations are produced. Overall there are 22 different tables that can be formed with each taking its name from the initial 2 pairs of letters in a particular commutation. To illustrate one form of this technique I will begin by splitting the Hebrew alphabet in half and putting one section on top of the other as can be seen below.

11	10	9	8	7	6	5	4	3	2	1
K	I	T	Ch	Z	V	H	D	G	B	A
L	M	N	S	O	P	Tz	Q	R	Sh	Th

Keep in mind that Hebrew in its hieroglyphic form is read from right to left, the opposite of English, which is why the preceding table appears to read backwards. The next step is to switch the last letter of the bottom line to the beginning of that line to produce 22 commutations:

11	10	9	8	7	6	5	4	3	2	1
K	I	T	Ch	Z	V	H	D	G	B	A
M	N	S	O	P	Tz	Q	R	Sh	Th	L

The reader should take notice that the letter Lamed (L) was switched from the 11th position in the bottom line to the first position thereby moving every other letter on that line over one space. If we now take the Hebrew word Ruach (RVCh) or "Spirit" and apply it to the shifted table the correspondences are R=D, V=Tz, and Ch=O, or RVCh = DTzO or "Detzau" which translates as "Ye shall cleave." This new word presents an interesting possibility for interpretation as cleave can mean either sticking together or tearing apart. From this we see Spirit expressed as either unity or separateness thereby suggesting that Spirit in fact has a ubiquitous nature that exists in both unity and duality. This particular method of the Tables of Tziruph is known as ALBTh or "Albath," deriving its name from the first pair of letters on both lines in the preceding table.

The second method of Temurah is referred to as AIQ BKR or "The Qabalah of the Nine Chambers." The name Nine Chambers derives from the method in which the Hebrew alphabet is divided into nine sections based on the similarities that exist in the numerical roots of the various letters. Below is a diagram of the nine chambers in which the theory behind the groupings will

QABALAH OF THE NINE CHAMBERS

300	30	3	200	20	2	100	10	1
Sh	L	G	R	K	B	Q	I	A
600	60	6	500	50	5	400	40	4
M Final	S	V	K Final	N	H	Th	M	D
900	90	9	800	80	8	700	70	7
Tz Final	Tz	T	P Final	P	Ch	N Final	O	Z

Illus. 5

become obvious.

As was the case with the previously mentioned system of Albath, the name AIQ BKR is also derived from the initial letters within the table, in this instance the three letters in both the first and second chambers on the top line going from right to left.

An example of where AIQ BKR can be utilized is in the Qabalistic operation of Squaring the Circle, an exercise in which the Higher meaning of the Pentagram (5 pointed Star) is revealed. The first step in this exercise is to draw a pentagram and then apply the letters of the word, ALHIM (The One in the Many), to each of the 5 points of the star beginning at the top point and proceeding in a clockwise direction.

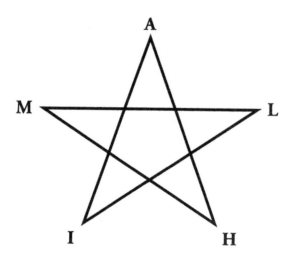

Illus. 6

Before I continue in my explanation of how to Square the Circle by using the Qabalah of the Nine Chambers, I would like to take a moment and discuss the significance of the word ALHIM which is commonly translated into English as "Elohim" and means "The One in the Many." This is a very unusual word in Hebrew in that ALHIM is a masculine plural of a feminine singular noun, namely ALHI, which is one of several ways of naming God in Hebrew. This gender bending of expressing a masculine concept with a feminine form is pure Qabalah because by mixing the basic elements of duality the balance and unity that underlies all Qabalistic thought is being presented for those who are willing to meditate upon this divine name. In the Bible, the Elohim were the Angelic legions of the Lord and were responsible for executing his will, thus each of the Elohim were an expression of "The One in the Many."

Now that the term ALHIM has been clarified, let's look at how one goes about Squaring a Circle in the Qabalah. Starting at the letter Lamed (L) which is ruled by the Astrological sign of Libra and therefore insinuates balance, let us then proceed in a counter-clockwise direction so the letters will be read in the reverse order of L, A, M, I, H. Next, the numerical values of each of these letters needs to be determined through the use of Gematria.

L (Lamed) = 30

A (Aleph) = 1

M (Mem) = 40

I (Yod) = 10

H (Heh) = 5

Applying the method of AIQ BKR will now show that the chamber containing Lamed also includes the letter Gimel (G) with a value of 3 and Shin (Sh) with a value of 300. In this instance, the value of Gimel will be exchanged with that of Lamed because by the rules of AIQ BKR the numerical values of letters within the same chamber are interchangeable. This same procedure must also be done for the letters Mem (M) and Yod (Y) as well so that the numerical totals of all the letters attributed to the points of the star are reduced to a single digit. Consulting the AIQ BKR table again will reveal that Mem (40) shares a chamber with Daleth (4). Likewise, Yod (10) shares a space with Aleph (1). Following the same procedure as with Lamed and Gimel, the adjusted values of the letters Mem and Yod become 4 and 1 respectively. As a result, the letters L, A, M, I, and H that are attributed to the points of the Pentagram now have the adjusted values of;

L (Lamed) = 3

A (Aleph) = 1

M (Mem) = 4

I (Yod) = 1

H (Heh) = 5

If these values are then looked upon as a five digit number, 31415, the result is equal to the value of Pi (π), the mathematical formula for computing the area of a circle. A square is then established over these 5 points of the star that have yielded the area of a circle by grouping the 4 lower points together to form the 4 elements of the material world (air, fire, earth, and water). The remaining fifth point at the top of the star then becomes symbolic of where the Spirit of God (ALHIM) enters into the form of man

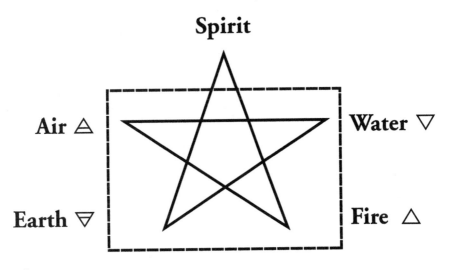

Illus. 7

(the Pentagram) to preside over the material realm.

At this point, the reader may be wondering, to what end is any of this? While extremely interesting, where is the practicality in all this manipulating of letters and numbers? Aleister Crowley answers this question in extremely witty fashion when he writes, "Truly there is no end to this wondrous science; and when the sceptic sneers, "With all these methods one ought to be able to make everything out of nothing," the Qabalist smiles back the sublime retort, "With these methods One did make everything out of nothing."

The way an Initiate's mind needs to work to perform the various machinations of the Qabalah and its associated systems is precisely the way the mind must work if the Magician is to find his or her True Will and appropriate place within the Universe. Being able to recognize and flow with the subtle levels of energy that exist all around is an acquired skill and the thought forms of The Qabalah are effectively a training program to develop such ability.

❖❖❖

CHAPTER III

ASTROLOGY

 simple definition of Astrology is that it can be likened to a costume drama in which a cast of characters known as Planets move through frequently revolving stage sets (the 12 Houses) and numerous wardrobe changes (the 12 Signs). Of course each of these planetary characters are really only aspects of a single character, specifically the person whose moment of birth is depicted in a natal Astrology chart. This elevation of an individual human being into the position of representing the unified consciousness of all the planets in the heavens is a decidedly Magickal perspective and one that clearly speaks of the connection between above and below, or God and Humanity. Following the movements of the planets therefore provides the Magician not only with valuable insights into his own character and that of others, but also with a more adept sense of timing in regards to the pursuit of the Great Work. The great 19th Century French Magus Eliphas Levi defined Magick as "Natural Science," and if one is inclined to view the Occult Arts as a system to facilitate a more effective awareness of the natural flow of things then what could possibly be a better strategy than familiarizing one's self with the patterns of how the heavens affect the earth before beginning a journey as important as that of living one's life?

In order to be able to use a study of the planets and their movements as a Magickal tool, it will first be necessary to become familiar with the elementary principles of Astrology, namely the Planets, the Signs, the Astrological Chart (the Houses), Aspects, Transits, and the cycles of the Moon.

PLANETS

An "Archetype" represents a mold or prototype from which all other subsequent models are derived. To a Jungian Psychologist, an archetype represents the various universal aspects of character that exist within each individual human being. Each of the planets in an Astrological chart are symbols for these archetypes, which the astute reader will notice from the ensuing descriptions derive a great deal from both Greek and Roman Mythology. In fact, for the serious student of Astrology there is no better method for studying the symbolism of the planets than to commit one's self to a thorough exploration of Ancient Mythology. What follows are some brief descriptions to give the reader a general idea of the concepts associated with each of the planets in an Astrology chart.

NEPTUNE ♆

For Ancient people the sea represented the great unknown, an immense, unfathomable abyss that surrounded the earth and led to the Kingdom of the Dead or "Hades." The sheer physical power of the Sea also impressed the Ancients, and in the archetype of the God Neptune both the mystical and material aspects of the ocean are expressed. In the Qabalah, Neptune signifies the Higher Power associated with the Supernal Spheres of both Kether and Chokmah on the Tree of Life, or the Divine connection between the heavens and the roots of material manifestation. At the same time the energies of Neptune are also ubiquitous and diffuse, thus the aura of this archetype is additionally linked with Psychic abilities and Mystical Expression. On a lower octave Neptune can signify illusion or escapism, and on that level this archetype is the ruler of many motion pictures, narcotics, and cult religions.

URANUS ♅

The original King of the Titans and father of the Gods, Uranus exemplified the unpredictable energy of pure creative genius. This association is drawn from the irony that although humanity gained all it possessed from the imagination and benevolence of the Gods, it was also true that these Higher Beings often behaved in mysterious, diabolical, and often destructive ways toward humans. While Neptune signified the soul of the sea or "The Great Subconscious," Uranus can be likened to the essence of pure creative fire; innovative, enlightening, useful, yet also potentially dangerous and destructive. In this day and age, Uranus is the ruling planetary force over unexpected happenings, revolutionary ideas and non-conformity, as well as technological innovations and the Internet.

SATURN ♄

The eldest son of Uranus, Saturn castrated his father in an attempt to curb the elder's often wanton and destructive flings. As a result, Saturn is looked upon as the bringer of structure to the world. This archetype is also associated with death because Saturn devoured his children at birth so as to never be deposed by an heir. The energy of Saturn is that which limits, restricts, and controls, with the end result in mind of producing a balanced structure based on a strong foundation. Subsequently, many Astrologer's refer to Saturn as "The Teacher." An example of the Saturnian influence is in his association as the God of Agriculture, a pursuit that utilizes and directs the bountiful energy of nature toward a productive goal.

JUPITER ♃

It was mentioned previously that Saturn devoured his children at birth, however, on the occasion of his son Jupiter's birth the baby's mother slipped a stone in swaddling clothes to her husband and then subsequently smuggled the small child to safety. When Jupiter eventually grew to manhood, he returned from his exile and overthrew his father ushering in the end of the rule of the Titans and the beginning the friendlier rule of the 12 Olympians. The personality of Jupiter was far more benevolent than that of his father and the new King ruled with wisdom and kindness only using the awesome power of his station when it was absolutely necessary. The archetype of Jupiter represents expansiveness, optimism, success, Higher Ideals, and benevolent strength.

MARS ♂

Mars was the Roman God of War and represents the pure energy of the warrior; brave, strong, violent, fierce, brutal, and resourceful, though not necessarily intelligent or discerning. In terms of its relation to human nature, the archetype of Mars symbolizes the raw force of will and ego unconcerned with consequences. On the body, Mars rules the head from which is derived the term "Headstrong."

THE SUN ☉

For the moment, I will leave behind Classical Mythology. This is due to the fact that the Astrological concept of the Sun is more developed than those characteristics usually associated with the Greek God of the Sun or "Apollo." In Astrology, the Sun is the most important of the planets for it represents the essence of the individual and marks the moment of birth. Just as the Sun is the center of our Solar System, in an Astrological chart it is the axle or center of the wheel and represents the whole person as opposed to the other planets which are but lesser aspects of the totality. By contrast, in Classical Mythology Apollo was not the most important of the Gods. Granted, he had his power, but ultimately he was no more exalted than the other Gods. The concept of the Sun as the ultimate planetary sphere is actually derived from the more ancient Solar religions of Syria and Egypt. According to these systems, nothing could exist without the life giving power of the Sun.

VENUS ♀

Born of the ocean from an oyster shell, Venus is associated with love, the reproductive powers of nature, and the highest vibration of womanhood. The Ancients looked upon her as the quintessential form of the Goddess embodying not only love, beauty, grace, and tenderness, but also the mystery, intuition, and power of the female archetype, hence Venus is additionally recognized as the force that governs Occult Wisdom. Because she represents the feminine energy that both yields and receives, Venus also serves to tempt strength and draw to us forces and situations that will be both protective and helpful.

MERCURY ☿

Known as the Messenger of the Gods, many forms have evolved over time for the figure of Mercury. Initially, he was the mischievous son of Jupiter and the "enfant terrible" of the Gods. From his youthful status came the role of the messenger because of the ancient custom of using the boys of the village or town to deliver messages. As he grew and became more worldly, the concept of Mercury developed from his accumulated experiences and we next see him become the creator of written language, commerce, and the Occult Sciences of Magick, Tarot, and Alchemy. Mercury's original boyishness and prankster qualities continued to survive despite his apparent maturity and accumulation of experience and we see evidence of this in his role as the patron God of Thieves. The archetype of Mercury in Astrology represents the mental processes and the formal abilities of communication and expression.

THE MOON ☽

While Venus represented the highest vibration of femininity, her younger sister symbolized by the Moon provides a metaphor regarding the different stages through which a woman will pass in her lifetime. This is illustrated in the Lunar Cycle when the Moon on its increase symbolizes the child or virgin (the Goddess Diana), the full moon symbolizes Motherhood (Ceres, the Earth Goddess) and the Moon on its decline signifies the Crone (the Goddess Hecate). Like her big sister, the Moon is also associated with the Occult because her shadowy, reflected light is believed to constitute the world of dreams and the Astral Plane. It is because of this mutable and mysterious quality that the Moon as an archetype represents our intuitions, feelings, and emotions, as well as the darker and more secretive aspects of human nature.

PLUTO ♇

Pluto was the ruler of the Kingdom of the Dead or "Hades." He was also known as the God of Wealth and presided over all the precious metals and gems within the Earth. Legend has it that Pluto was the owner of a Magickal Helmet as well, of which it was said that whoever wore it would be rendered invisible. In Astrology, Pluto symbolizes death and transformation. These regenerative powers also distinguish Pluto as the God of Mystical Sexuality, whereby through surrender to the symbolic death of the orgasm, a state of Divine Union can be achieved between previously separate elements of consciousness.

SIGNS

Now that the reader has been introduced to the various planetary characters, let us now take a look at the different costumes or "Signs" in which these characters may be outfitted.
I will begin with a brief philosophical digression because some basic concepts need to be explained in order to understand why the Signs are associated with the four basic elements.

The basic quality of the Universe is Unity; however, the human mind operates on the principle of duality. In order to comprehend existence, human beings need to be able to make comparisons. For example, the female principle within humanity can only be fully understood in relation to the male principle. It is possible through a Mystical process to join these seemingly opposing principles of male and female to reform unity, yet the more mundane natural course is for the two to combine and create a third. The Ancient magicians referred to this triad as "The Three Mother Elements," composed of fire, air, and water, or the three possible states in which one can experience the Universe; Being, Non-Being, and Becoming. From this trinity of active elements, a passive factor is then consolidated to solidify a physical reality in the form of earth, whereby a four part elemental system is created which allows for an infinite number of combinations to evolve. The 12 Signs of the Zodiac are then subsequently grouped together within this four part elemental system (fire, air, water, and earth) with each elemental classification containing three signs that correspond to the three Mother Elements. Thus for the element of fire (which corresponds to creative energy) the three Signs are Aries, Sagittarius, and Leo, which each relate respectively to the Hermetic notions of Fiery (or Cardinal), Watery (or Mutable), and Airy (or Fixed) qualities of fire. Another way of explaining this would be to say that Aries is the Fiery or most violent and active manifestation of fire, an example in nature being lightning. Sagittarius would then be the Watery or most passive and controllable form of the element, an example being the use of fire in a domestic setting. Finally, Leo would be the Airy or Highest Spiritual form of the concept of fire and would be exemplified by the heat and warmth of the Sun.

Keeping this basic elemental structure in mind, let's now look at some of the other characteristics of the three Fire Signs.

ARIES   ♈

The planet Mars rules this sign, and the costume of Aries is the perfect outfit for the warrior. The Ram is the animal attribution and the energy of Aries is direct, forceful, impetuous, and passionate, with the sign being symbolic of physical activity, aggressiveness, and initiative.

SAGITTARIUS   ♐

Represented by the Centaur (a half-man, half-horse creature) aiming his bow and arrow towards the sky, the sign of Sagittarius is the native environment for the planet Jupiter and symbolizes adventure, optimism, generosity, travel, higher learning, philosophy, and prophecy.

LEO ♌

The animal associated with Leo is the Lion, and the planet ruling this sign is the Sun. The sign of Leo symbolizes courage, leadership, the performing arts, public attention, love, compassion, strength, and the power of the heart.

WATER SIGNS

The Water Signs represent the emotions

CANCER

Symbolized by the Crab, Cancer represents the fiery (Cardinal) aspects of water. In nature, this active quality is exemplified by the rain, streams, and rivers. The Moon is the planet that rules Cancer so this sign is also synonymous with the subconscious, intuition, and nurturing. Because of their sometimes vulnerable emotional make-up, Cancer natives are often capable of behaving very much like crabs by either withdrawing into seclusion within the environments they have constructed for themselves or reacting aggressively.

PISCES ♓

Pisces or "The Fishes" is the Watery (or Mutable) aspect of water represented by the reflective, passive qualities of wells and pools.

The planet Neptune rules this sign, hence Pisces is the romantic of the Zodiac as well as the most Psychic of all the Signs. Because of its Neptunian affiliation, Pisces can often become quite distracted and lapse into a fantasy world where illusion and escapism predominate.

SCORPIO ♏

Scorpio represents the Airy (or Fixed) aspect of Water and is exemplified by the sea. Symbolized by the Scorpion on its lower octave and by the Eagle on its higher octave, Scorpio is ruled by the planet Pluto and subsequently signifies the more intense side of human nature. Due also to its association with Pluto, Scorpio is additionally the sign that rules desire, sex, and death.

AIR SIGNS

The Air Signs symbolize the Mental Processes

LIBRA ♎

Symbolized by either the scales or the setting Sun on the horizon, the sign of Libra signifies balance and harmony. Libra also represents the fiery or active aspects of air, which is expressed in nature through both the power of the wind and the ubiquitous quality of the atmosphere surrounding the earth. The planet Venus rules this sign so the energy of Libra is very much about beauty, harmony, and union, though on a lower level this sign can also be characterized by laziness and indecision. An important thing to keep in mind about Libra is that while the sign does signify balance, it can also in varying degrees be about aggressiveness as well as compromise depending on what factors are necessary to restore equilibrium.

GEMINI Ⅱ

One of the two home environments of the planet Mercury, Gemini is symbolized by the twins and exemplifies the duality required for the human mind to be able to comprehend its circumstances. This sign represents the watery or mutable aspects of air, a quality which can best be illustrated by the act of respiration, a process which utilizes the power of air through assimilation in order to fuel human intelligence. The sign of Gemini is also characterized by a love of variety, adaptability, communication, conversation, new experiences, curiosity, and information.

AQUARIUS ♒

Aquarius represents the airy or fixed aspect of air and serves as a harmonizing middle ground between the other two Air Signs. The mythological association for this sign is Ganymede, the Trojan Prince who was the water bearer of the Gods. This correspondence is particularly profound because when the nature of Air becomes sufficiently fixed, it coagulates into water bearing clouds. The planet Uranus rules this Sign and the character of Aquarius is associated with freedom, innovation, creativity, eccentricity, rebelliousness, and revolution.

EARTH SIGNS

The Earth Signs are associated with
the material world

CAPRICORN ♑

Capricorn is the fiery essence of the earth, or its formative force
exemplified by mountains and volcanoes. This is the environment
that favors both ambition and authority, yet because it is ruled by
Saturn, Capricorn also represents the need for patience with the
structures in our lives if we hope to satisfy our ambitions. On a
lower octave this sign symbolized by the goat can also signify
pessimism, restriction, and the lower vibrational elements of
Spiritual practice.

VIRGO ♍

Virgo or "The Virgin" is the watery, passive aspect of earth that
yields itself in the form of fields and pastures that can be cultivated
by other energies. Virgo represents the second sign that offers a
home to the planet Mercury, yet unlike Gemini, which is the
Mercurial energy that transmits, Virgo is the essence of Mercury
that discerns and utilizes. Where communication and socializing
would be the Gemini ray of Mercury, formal systems such as
language and the Healing Arts (Virgo is the sign of the Nurse)
would be the Virgoan ray of the Messenger Planet. Other qualities
associated with this sign are organization, maintenance, and
problem solving, although on a lower octave these qualities could
deteriorate into rigidity and excessive criticism.

TAURUS ♉

Taurus or "The Bull" represents the airy or fixed aspect of earth which combines the fiery and watery qualities of the other two earth signs into a stable pattern that could best be interpreted as the essence of labor or cultivation. Representing the other sign besides Libra that is ruled by the planet Venus, Taurus translates the Venusian ray into sensuality, luxury, and a deep, abiding appreciation for the beauty of nature. Other qualities associated with this sign are stability, strength, practicality, and patience, though on a lower level Taurus resists change and can represent close-mindedness, stubbornness, and stagnation.

THE ASTROLOGICAL CHART

(The Houses)

Now that the basic symbolism of both the Planets and the Signs has been discussed, the next step will be to place these symbols in a heavenly context so the progress of their relative relationships can be mapped. Before I begin describing this heavenly map, otherwise known as an Astrological Chart, let's first examine some elementary points concerning the make-up of the heavens.

It is a popular misconception that the Solar System is shaped like a sphere with the planets suspended therein like raisins in a pudding. The actual fact of the matter is that the Solar System is in the form of a flat disc and the planets all revolve around the Sun on approximately the same basic plane. It is also important to realize that this disc is not shaped like a circle, but rather an elliptic due to the fact that all the planets are at varying distances from the Sun. With this in mind, the circular format used for an Astrological Chart is really an abstraction organized primarily for clarity and convenience rather than physical accuracy.

Based on the Geometric form of a circle, the conventional Astrological Chart incorporates the mathematical regularity of this basic shape to attempt to create an organized and coherent map of the heavens. The first characteristic of this map that I will examine takes its cue from one of the elementary tenets of Geometry, namely that the sum of all the possible angles in a circle total 360 degrees. From this bit of information it can then be deduced that the 12 divisions or "Houses" of an Astrological Chart each contain 30 degrees. (360 divided by 12 = 30)

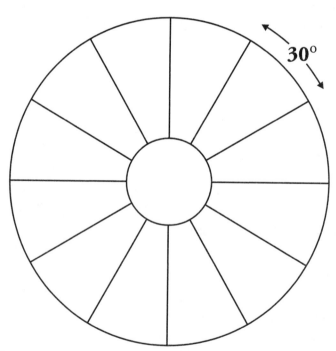

Illus. 8

These 12 sections can then each be divided into 3 smaller parts called "Decanates" (equaling 10 degrees) and 6 even smaller parts called "Quinaries"(equaling 5 degrees). A full Astrological Chart consisting of 360 degrees would therefore contain 72 quinaries (360 divided by 5 = 72), each of which is in turn ruled by a different Angelic being collectively known as "The Shemhamphorasch." This point concerning the Angelic names and their relevance to the Zodiac is not particularly important at this stage in the discussion, although further ahead in Chapter 11, I will explain how to utilize these names in the construction of a Birthday Talisman.

The next item regarding the form of the Astrological Chart concerns the smaller central circle surrounded by the 12 Houses. This section is meant to symbolize the essence or "Spirit" of the person to whom the chart refers as they witness the movement of the heavens around the image of their incarnation. This central vantage point is sometimes referred to as "The 13th House" and is symbolic of a greater consciousness (the Higher Self) presiding over its individual components.

The diameter that divides the circle into equal upper and lower halves is the next aspect of the chart I will discuss as this demarcation is meant to represent the horizon with the left side corresponding to the "Ascendant," or the constellation rising at the time of birth, and the right side corresponding to the "Descendent," or the constellation setting at the time of birth. This division of the circle into upper and lower halves is also intended to signify the public and private arenas of a person's life, with the upper section corresponding to the public self and the lower section referring to the private self. The circle can also be divided vertically into equal halves and the point on the circumference touched by the upper radius of this diameter is a spot known as "The Mid-heaven" or the highest point in the chart. The lower radius of this vertical diameter touches another point on the circumference known as "The Imum Celi" or the lowest point in the chart. The Mid-heaven and the sign associated with it represents how the individual will move forward in their life and the Imum Celi along with its respective sign will indicate the inner style motivating the energy exhibited at the Mid-heaven.

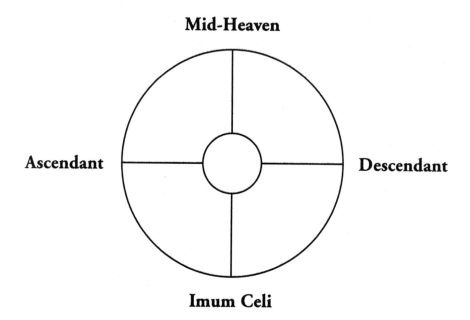

Illus. 9

Another concept that is important to understand regarding the Astrological Chart is that the planets move around the circle in a counter-clockwise direction, the exception being when some of the planets periodically go retrograde and appear to be moving backwards or clockwise around the circle. Of course no planet ever actually reverses its direction, rather it is just that the Earth moves so much faster than the other planets that it makes them appear as if they were going backwards. A similar illusion occurs when an express train passes a local and the slower train appears as though it were going backwards.

The general effect upon a planet's energies when it goes retrograde is that the qualities associated with that sphere will become reversed or muddled. Probably the most well known retrograde effect is when Mercury reverses its apparent direction 3 times a year. Each of these periods lasts for 3 weeks and during this time there are often unexpected difficulties with both communication and travel. The ratio of the time Mercury spends going retrograde in comparison to when it is direct is very close to the ratio of the amount of time a human being spends sleeping as opposed to being awake. As a result, Mercury retrograde is an excellent time to spend in review of projects that have ended up being delayed, just as it is often a good idea to take a fresh look at our daily problems after a good night's rest. Another example of a retrograde effect would be money or relationship matters becoming delayed when Venus reverses her direction.

HOUSES

Each of the 12 sections or "Houses" of the Astrological Chart provide different backdrops for the planets and the signs. Probably the easiest way to comprehend the effect of the Houses in a chart is to imagine that, like the planets, they each represent a different element of the person's life in relation to the full chart. Following is a diagram of the 12 Houses and the associated facets of human behavior they represent.

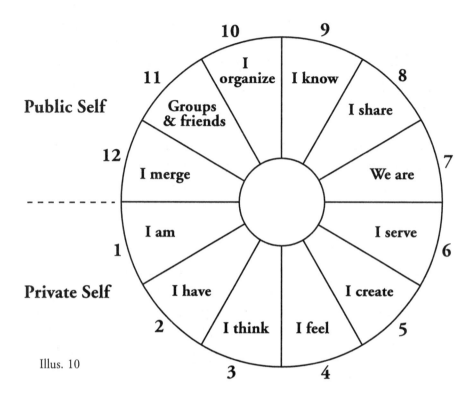

Illus. 10

Each House also has a Sign which is its natural ruler.

1st House - Aries	♈	7th House - Libra	♎
2nd House - Taurus	♉	8th House - Scorpio	♏
3rd House - Gemini	♊	9th House - Sagittarius	♐
4th House - Cancer	♋	10th House- Capricorn	♑
5th House - Leo	♌	11th House - Aquarius	♒
6th House - Virgo	♍	12th House - Pisces	♓

Illus. 11

The above pairings of Signs and Houses correspond to what is known as a natural chart with a First House of Aries. These pairings will shift as the wheel is rotated to accommodate for different birth locations and times. An example of this can be seen in my birth chart where Libra is matched with my First House, Scorpio with my Second House, and so on.

Now that the reader has a general idea of the Houses, let's look at some additional information associated with each of these slices of the Astrological Pie.

The First House
This house represents the identity and temperament you project to the world, as well as your physical characteristics and health.

The Second House
The Second House represents an individual's possessions and their ability to increase them. On a deeper level this house also describes one's sense of self worth.

The Third House
This House deals with the mental abilities of the individual and their style of communication as well as relationships with siblings, short trips, and those acquaintances with whomever one has an intellectual rather than an emotional relationship.

The Fourth House
The lowest point in the Astrological Chart, this House describes one's symbolic foundations; home, parents (specifically the Mother), family, and childhood. The 4th House has also been said to describe the conditions to be expected at the end of life as well as the circumstances of one's death.

The Fifth House

This is the House of Creativity and describes the fun-loving side of the individual and their amorous affairs. Additionally, Children are also a Fifth House issue.

The Sixth House

The Sixth house describes the routines we follow and how we function on a daily basis. It also shows our work, work environment, and how we take care of our health. Pets are traditionally associated with the 6th House.

The Seventh House

The Seventh House is the environment that governs an individual's partnerships. It is known as the House of Marriage, yet business partnerships and our open enemies also figure into the realm encompassed by the 7th House.

The Eighth House

This is the House of Death and Resurrection, agony and ecstasy, sex, shared resources, other people's money, and inheritances.

The Ninth House

The Ninth House pertains to Higher issues such as Philosophy, Religion, Spirituality, our Teachers and Mentors, long journeys of great importance, Higher Education, the Great Outdoors, and Publishing.

The Tenth House

The highest point in the Astrological Chart, this House affects career, reputation, and social status. In some cases this environment also describes the character and influence of the father.

The Eleventh House

Friends, fondest hopes and dreams, how one relates to groups, and the groups that one associates with are all attributed to the 11th House.

The Twelfth House

This is the House of the Secret Self, that part of us that exists when we are all alone. This is also the house of restrictions and confinement, secrecy, and all matters of intrigue. The Twelfth House also represents Higher Spiritual union and the merging of the individual with the collective.

ASPECTS

An "Aspect" in Astrology refers to the relationship between two or more Planets in a chart. The size of the angle that separates the planets as well as the elements governing the signs the planets are in will determine the nature of the conversation between the spheres involved. Generally speaking, there are five major aspects or types of communication that planets may engage in.

Opposition ($\mathcal{S}$ 180°)

Planets in opposition are 180 degrees apart and like the name of this aspect implies, they are directly opposite each other in the sky. Depending on the Planets and Signs involved, this aspect can play out as either a tug of war or a balanced ride on a seesaw.

Trine ($\triangle$ 120°)

Planets involved in a trine are 120 degrees apart in Signs ruled by the same element, hence this aspect signifies a nice, easy flow of energy.

Square (□ 90°)

Planets in a square are 90 degrees apart and situated in Signs whose elements are somewhat incompatible (Fire & Water or Air & Earth). This is the angle of both creativity and conflict, hence this aspect will point to an obstacle which needs to be overcome to facilitate further growth.

Sextile (✳ 60°)

Planets in a sextile are 60 degrees apart and situated in Signs ruled by complementary elements (Fire & Air or Earth & Water). A Sextile represents potential energy that will only be accessible through some form of concerted effort.

Conjunction (☌ 0-8°)

When two or more planets are at the same degree in the same Sign they are said to be "Conjunct." The effect of this aspect can be likened to locking a pair of individuals in a closet together and then telling them to work out their differences. As with the opposition, the outcome of this aspect can be either rough or easy depending on the planets and signs involved.

TRANSITS

Transits refer to the daily movements of the planets and how they relate to the positions of the planets in an individual's Birth Chart. For example, Neptune in my Natal Chart is located at 29 degrees Libra and at this very moment Mercury is also currently in the sky at 29 degrees Libra, thus I am having a Mercury transit over my Neptune. This would mean that the unique energy of Mercury is activating the Neptunian influence I was born with. Coincidentally enough, this is an excellent combination for doing exactly what I am currently engaged in, namely writing (which is Mercurial) about Occult Practices (which are Neptunian) while both planets are in a sign (Libra) that signifies balance and exalts Literary pursuits.

THE MOON CYCLE

While the Sun takes approximately 1 month to pass through a Sign, the Moon manages to do it in roughly 2 and a half days. In the section on the Planets, the Moon was described as representing our feelings and emotions, therefore by being aware of the daily movements of the Lunar Sphere the Magician can gain a deeper understanding of the current emotional and energetic landscape, both within the self and for the world at large. A complete Lunar Cycle consists of the Moon making one full trip around the Astrological Chart with this trip taking approximately one month during which time the Sphere's progress is divided into four stages or "Quarters".

The First Quarter/ New Moon

This is when the Moon and the Sun are together or "Conjunct" in the sky. As this first phase develops, the Moon will begin to move further away from the Sun so that more of her will become visible in the form of an increasing crescent shape. The New Moon symbolizes new beginnings and is an excellent time to embark upon a new project or relationship.

The Second Quarter

This second phase begins once the Moon has moved 90 degrees away from the Sun and appears as a Half-Moon in the sky. The Second Quarter signifies the development of life and the approaching fruition of those things started on the New Moon.

The Third Quarter/ Full Moon ○

This is when the Sun and the Moon are opposite each other in the sky and the Moon appears as a glowing circle of light. The Full Moon symbolizes the culmination of plans and the maturing of the situations initiated at the beginning of the cycle.

The Fourth Quarter ◐

The Fourth Quarter is when the Moon is on her decrease and the current cycle is coming to a close. This is the completion phase and represents a time to assess the results of our efforts from the New Moon in order to regroup and prepare for the next cycle.

As she passes through each of the Signs, the Moon will take on the vibration of each respective environment. Following is a list of the general moods that may be prevalent as the Moon passes through the different Signs of the Zodiac.

ARIES - One feels aggressive and impulsive. A good time to start new projects.

TAURUS - This is a time of complacency, sensuality, and material concerns.

GEMINI - A sociable and active time

CANCER - The native environment of the Moon and a time for nurturing, home, and family.

LEO - This is when one desires to be the center of attention and be recognized for our accomplishments.

VIRGO - A time to organize and direct one's concerns toward maintenance and personal health.

LIBRA - A good time for partnerships and to regain inner balance.

SCORPIO - A time of intense emotions and a good period to engage in any sort of investigative work.

SAGITTARIUS - This is a time when people are fun loving and optimistic. Also a good time to promote ideas and pursue Higher learning.

CAPRICORN - A time for following the rules and taking care of business. Be careful of pessimism or depression.

AQUARIUS - A time for freedom, rebellion, innovation, and independence.

PISCES - People are vulnerable and compassionate. Psychic abilities become highly tuned.

THE VOID-OF-COURSE MOON

This is a period in which the Moon has encountered all the aspects in a particular sign and for the remaining time in that environment she is essentially adrift with nothing to relate to until passing into the next Sign. A voided Moon can last for a few minutes or several days depending on where the various planets are located. During this time people often experience feeling ungrounded or disconnected and it is not recommended to make plans of any sort for it is believed that strategies formulated when the Moon is void-of-course will ultimately amount to nothing. On the other hand, a void-of-course Moon is an excellent time for Psychic readings or gaining clarity concerning a past situation because of the lack of extenuating energies that would cloud judgment.

As one may imagine, Astrology is a vast and complex field with everything that I have written up until now representing merely the most basic information on the subject. In order to give the reader an idea of just how this information can be applied, I have included the Birth Chart of Aleister Crowley (Illus. 12) from which I will briefly discuss some of the more obvious aspects.

The first aspect in Crowley's chart that catches my attention is Uranus (♅) at 19 degrees Leo (♌) in the First House opposing Saturn (♄) at 19 degrees Aquarius (♒) in the Seventh House. The Planetary archetype of innovation, creativity, and eccentricity, Uranus is the closest planet to Crowley's Leo Ascendant and certainly explains both his infamously flamboyant public persona as well as his relentlessly creative nature that found its expression in his prolific literary output and tireless pursuit of the Great Work. The other half of this opposition is Saturn, the planetary archetype of structure, which is in the egalitarian sign of Aquarius in the Seventh house, the portion of the chart that influences both partnerships and enemies. This is significant in that throughout his entire life Crowley was always in the ironic position of being demonized for openly challenging the conventional social order, while at the same time embodying a learned and structured intellectual approach to this rebellion that pre-dated much of our current progressive New Age thinking. The Uranus/Saturn

Aleister Crowley
Natal Chart

October 12, 1875
11:16 pm
Leamington Spa, ENG

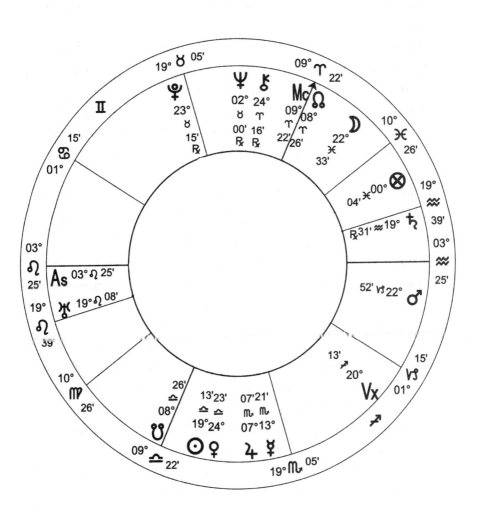

opposition in Crowley's chart is further colored by a Uranus/Sun sextile and a Sun/Saturn trine. Both of these aspects originate from the Sun (☉) at 19 degrees Libra (♎) in the Fourth House, and from this balanced foundation the Uranus/Sun sextile represents Crowley's innovative, Occult nature while the Sun/Saturn trine speaks of the solidity and lasting influence of his innovative thought.

The second point I will discuss involves Crowley's Fourth House, the environment that describes the symbolic foundations of home and family. For those who may not know, Crowley was raised by fanatical Religious Fundamentalists, an upbringing that forced him to memorize the Bible as a child and eventually grow to despise Christianity as a man. That his Fourth House is divided almost equally between the Signs of Libra (balance) and Scorpio (transformation) would explain Crowley's obsession as a Spiritual Explorer, a drive which no doubt evolved from his experiencing the lower octave of Organized Religion when he was a boy. With Venus (♀) and the Sun in the Libra half of the Fourth house, Crowley had the intuition to perceive the grains of Higher Truth lost amidst his parent's misguided notions, while with Jupiter (♃) and Mercury (☿) in the Scorpio (♏) portion of that same House he also had the intelligence and expansiveness to embrace the full range of Mystical experience after he transcended his parent's dogmatic beliefs.

To close this chapter on Astrology, I will speak briefly about how an Initiate may use this branch of Magickal language in his or her pursuit of the Great Work. What follows is a short list of a few basic practices that, if pursued daily, will serve to expand one's Magickal understanding.

1 - Buy a Daily Planetary Guide and follow the Moon Cycles. Within a few short weeks you will begin to start to feel how the Moon changes her qualities as she passes through the Signs.

2 - Experiment by consciously beginning projects during a New Moon and then noticing how far you have progressed by the Full Moon.

3 - Have a Birth Chart done either through a private Astrologer or an Astrological Service and then follow the daily movements of the Planets as they transit through your Natal Chart. On significant days try to be mindful concerning the influences of the particular planets involved.

4 - Consciously try to make important appointments on Astrologically favorable days, though you will eventually notice that beneficial meetings often synchronistically occur on such days.

In short, consciously try to use Astrological information to put yourself in the right place at the right time so as to maximize the probability that you will be exercising your True Will and Higher Magickal Power.

❖❖❖

CHAPTER IV

THE TAROT

HERE are two different ways of looking at the Tarot. The first approach is to use the Cards as an Oracle, or as Webster's Collegiate Dictionary mundanely states, as "a deck of picture cards used for fortune telling." This initial view expresses the popular idea of the Cards held by the general public, although it is not the perspective this book will take. For the purposes of this work I will examine another way of looking at the Tarot, namely as an illustrated book of Spiritual knowledge that contains a complex language of symbols drawn from the Qabalah and Astrology as well as Egyptian, Greek, and Roman Mythology.

The Ancient Magicians attributed a pair of Divine Intelligences to the Tarot. The first of these Higher Beings was Mercury, the Messenger of the Gods in Greek Mythology who was believed to be the inventor of the Cards as well as the Esoteric Practices of both Magick and Alchemy. In the Qabalistic scheme of things Mercury is attributed to the 8th Sphere on the Tree of Life known as Hod or "Splendor." Ruling the mental processes along with the male sexual (or creative) energy, Hod is generally believed to represent the lower material manifestation of the Supernal Sphere of Chokmah or "Wisdom." The planet attributed to Chokmah is Neptune, and in the preceding chapter on

Astrology Neptune was said to represent both the Divine Initiating Force and Psychic power. This association to the Psychic realm is an apt one since Neptune is the God of the Sea and the energy of the ocean is both diffuse and ubiquitous, coinciding perfectly with the mysterious and often non-specific qualities of Psychic impressions. From these analogies, the Ancients subsequently saw the Tarot as an attempt by the God Mercury to create a codified system through which to render the vagueness of the psychic or "Neptunian" realm into an intelligible language comprehensible to the human mind.

The second Divine Intelligence attributed by the Ancient Adepts to the Tarot was the Angel HRU, the entity who guarded the sanctity of the oracle invented by Mercury so that the powers of this system would not be abused. The Hebrew spelling of this Angelic name is, HRV, and concealed within these three letters is a poignant Qabalistic mystery.

The first letter of HRV is H or "Heh," the fifth letter of the Hebrew alphabet that translates as "a window." The numerical value of Heh is 5, so it can therefore be correlated to the 5 pointed star or "Pentagram" that signifies earthly reality or "The Microcosm" to the Qabalistic Magician. The last letter of HRV is V or "Vav," the sixth letter of the Hebrew alphabet that translates as "a nail." The numerical value of Vav is 6 so it can be correlated to the 6 pointed star or "Hexagram," the Star of Love that symbolizes the Heavens or "The Macrocosm." The remaining letter of HRV is the middle R or "Resh," the 20th letter of the Hebrew alphabet that means "a head" and whose numerical value is 200.

A synthesis of the preceding information would reveal that through the Angelic name of HRV the Tarot can be described as a system for connecting the Higher Psychic Energy of Neptune (symbolized by the phallic nail and the Hexagram representing the Heavens) to the material realm symbolized by the Pentagram to create "a window" (Heh) of enlightenment within the head (Resh) or perceptions of each individual.

The numerical total of the name HRV is 211 (H=5, R=200, V=6), and by using the Qabalistic technique of Gematria (comparing words with the same numerical value) a pair of interesting associations are revealed. The first is the Hebrew word, HARH or "a lightning flash," the flash obviously referring to the enlightenment gained by joining the Pentagram and Hexagram into a unified perception as previously illustrated within the name HRV. The second correspondence does not involve a direct comparison to another word with the same numerical value, but rather takes form as a result of reducing the number 211 to 2 + 11 or 13, the numerical value of the Hebrew words AHBH (Love) and AChD (Unity), a pair of words that also speak of the joining of the Pentagram (the Earth or the Mother) with the Hexagram (the Heavens or the Father) to gain a unified perception or "enlightenment."

THE STRUCTURE OF THE TAROT

The Tarot consists of 78 picture cards that are divided into two sections known as the Minor Arcana or "Suits" and the Major Arcana or "Trumps." The Minor Arcana contains 56 cards and is divided into 4 groups known respectively as Wands, Cups, Swords, and Pentacles. Each of these groups or "Suits" contains 14 cards numbered from Ace (or 1) to 10 with 4 additional Court Cards (Page, Knight, Queen, and King). It is generally believed that the Minor Arcana is primarily an oracle pertaining to material matters, so in keeping with my original stated purpose of this book focusing on the Tarot as a book of Esoteric Wisdom I will limit my analysis of the cards to the Major Arcana or "Trumps" as that section of the Tarot contains the Spiritual symbolism that will serve our purposes.

Having thus stated my intention to focus on the Major Arcana, I will now respectfully ask for the reader's indulgence while I make a brief digression to discuss a very important Esoteric concept that is the underlying reason for how the 4 suits of the Minor Arcana are organized. The concept I am alluding to is derived from the Qabalah and expressed in a Hebrew term known as "Tetragrammaton." This word denotes the ineffable name of God (that which is beyond expression) and is spelled, IHVH (Yod, Heh, Vav, Heh) which is literally unpronounceable in Hebrew due to the fact that it contains no vowel indicator or "dogesh," although on a Spiritual level this name is not to be uttered because of the awesome, all encompassing power it represents.

Aside from being a name of God, the Tetragrammaton is also a Magickal formula which Aleister Crowley describes as being "of most universal aspect, as all things are necessarily comprehended in it." In order to explain the universal aspect Crowley attributes to IHVH it will be necessary to analyze each of its 4 letters individually.

I = Yod, the tenth letter of the Hebrew alphabet which translates as "a finger," or more specifically "the index finger." The phallic connotation is quite obvious and the role of this first letter in the formula is that of the initiating force in the universe, or the Divine Male Energy.

H = Heh, the fifth letter of the Hebrew alphabet which translates as "a window," and represents the potential, receptivity, and openness of the archetypal Mother or Divine Feminine Energy.

V = Vav, the sixth letter of the Hebrew alphabet which translates as "a nail." V represents the Son, or the third created from the union of the initial two elements of the formula with the meaning of "a nail" signifying the potency of the Father rejuvenated through the Son.

H = the letter Heh, seen previously in the formula as representing the Mother, although repeated as the final letter it is meant to signify the daughter or the potential of the Mother perpetuated so that the cycle of creation may continue.

Each of the letters included in the Tetragrammaton can then subsequently be applied to a specific suit in the Tarot, thus making the Cards a metaphor of the Divine Creative Intelligence.

Letter	Suit	Element	Properties
I	Wands	Fire	Initiating creative energy
H	Cups	Water	Infinite potential or the receptacle which gives form
V	Swords	Air	The rejuvinated energy of the Divine in Earthly form
H	Pentacles	Earth	The manifested fruits of the Earth

Illus. 13

The Magickal concept of the Tetragrammaton is also illustrated in the organization of the Court Cards within each suit with I corresponding to The Kings, H corresponding to The Queens, V corresponding to The Knights, and the final H corresponding to The Pages.

In the older Tarot decks, the Pages were originally Princesses (which would seem more logical in a Tetragrammatic sense) although in his rectified Tarot (the deck that will be used in this book) A.E. Waite has changed the Princesses to Pages. I believe this represents a Hermetic riddle and my reasoning takes its cue from the pronounced effeminate appearances of the Pages in the Waite/Smith deck. To my mind, this bisexual presentation of the Pages is a clue that they are really supposed to be androgynous and embody the qualities of both male and female. This androgyny is then in turn supposed to be a metaphor of the Great Work, an activity by which the Magician attempts to unify and balance the opposing aspects of duality within his or her earthly incarnation (represented by the Daughter of IHVH which corresponds to the Pages of the Tarot). This theory is further supported by the fact that the Pages (or Princesses) are traditionally associated with the Earth Sphere of Malkuth on the Tree of Life.

THE MAJOR ARCANA

Now that the underlying Magickal concept of the Suits of the Tarot has been discussed, I will get back on track and begin looking at the Major Arcana or "Trumps" of the Tarot.

Consisting of 22 cards numbered from 0 to 21, the Major Arcana is sometimes referred to as "The Fool's Journey" owing to the fact that the first of the Trumps which is numbered "0" is named "The Fool" and is meant to represent each of us on our journey through life as we evolve and experience the different archetypes that exist within us (symbolized by the other 21 cards).

As the first card of the Major Arcana, The Fool represents each of us on our journey through life. The number assigned to The Fool is 0, which would seem appropriate in that 0 is in essence a blank slate upon which an impression needs to be made before it can be determined to be one thing or another. The Fool represents being open to unexpected influences and new beginnings and speaks to the need to abandon what is outmoded in order to embrace what is new. The card depicts a gaily-attired young man about to step off of a cliff. This young man is traveling light and doesn't seem to be very concerned with where he's going. The seeming naivety of The Fool is essentially the basis for what is known in Zen Buddhism as "No-mind" that state of enlightened consciousness that symbolizes being totally present, non-judgmental, and flexible to the flow of the Universe.

In the upper right corner of the image of The Fool a white sun is shining that is meant to symbolize the Divine Light coming from the One Infinite Creator. The purity and power of this energy is further reflected in the white rose The Fool holds in his left hand (corresponding to the Sphere of Chesed on the Tree of Life which rules an individual's ability to receive and embrace the world) as well as in the white shirt he wears under his tunic, of which the right arm is exposed (corresponding to the Sphere of Geburah on the Tree of Life which rules an individual's ability to move forward and manifest one's desires). It is also significant that The Fool is holding a wooden staff (symbolizing the element of fire) in his right hand implying that his actions will always be pure if he adheres to the guidance of the white light. The repeating red and yellow circular pattern on The Fool's outer tunic is the Qabalistic symbol for the Spirit of the Higher Self and shows the relaxed attitude of the young man as the surface manifestation of the pure consciousness coming from the Higher source of the white sun. In the lower right of the picture a little white dog scampers along beside The Fool providing a Hermetic reference to the Greek God Mercury, inventor of the Tarot. This attribution derives from the Egyptian God Thoth (the equivalent of Mercury) and his sometimes companion the dog-headed monkey Cynocephalus. The relationship of this pair alternated between being complementary and comically difficult, hence the reference is intended to be symbolic of how some things the universe deals us are an annoyance, yet the greater plan is always one looking toward evolution and growth.

The last aspect of The Fool I want to discuss refers to the satchel suspended on the end of the stick he is carrying. The original edition of the Waite/Smith deck had this small bag decorated with both the Eye of Horus and a Falcon's Head, yet subsequent editions of the deck only included the Falcon's Head.

Both symbols speak to the regeneration of the God or hero who has emerged from a journey of Initiation similar to what The Fool is about to embark upon as he launches into his journey through the Major Arcana.

THE MAGICIAN.

© 1971 U.S. Games

The image on the card of The Magician is that of a Mage with his Magickal implements spread out on a table before him. These implements are the objects associated with the four suits of the Tarot and their elemental correspondences represent the creative potential of the material world. Standing over these objects, the Magician signifies the power of Spirit or "The Higher Self" presiding over the material realm, a concept revealed in the chapter on The Qabalah as being the Higher Mystery of the 5 pointed star or "Pentagram." The Infinity sign hovering above The Magician's head is the Esoteric Sign of Life or the Sign of the Holy Spirit and represents the birth of Christ in Gnostic

Christianity. That The Magician is simultaneously pointing both above and below is to signify that he is a conduit between the heavens and the earth, yet it should also be noted that in the hand he is extending upwards towards the heavens The Magician is holding a wand, although this implement bears no similarity to the type of wand associated with the suit of wands in the Tarot. What the Magician holds is about the manifestation of the Magickal Power of the Higher Self, which through the archetype of the Mage will unite with the potential for form to create what will eventually evolve into The Fool's Journey. The red cloak of The Magician is symbolic of the Alchemical element of Sulphur and further elucidates the Mage's ability to initiate catalytic change, while his white shirt is representative of the purity of his intent. Around the waist of The Magician is a blue serpent cincture (or belt) in which the animal is depicted as swallowing its own tail. This is a spin off on an ancient symbol for eternity known as a "Urobos" and illustrates the flowing universal source of the Mage's power. In the foreground of the card there is a mingling of rose bushes and lilies that are symbolic of the earthly cycle of life and death. There is also a bower of roses hanging above The Magician and this represents Occult knowledge for the rose is the flower of Venus and the Goddess of Love is also the patroness of Esoteric wisdom.

THE HIGH PRIESTESS

© 1971 U.S. Games

The card of The High Priestess is attributed to the 13th Pathway on the Tree of Life that connects the heart Sphere of Tiphareth to the Crown Sphere of Kether while passing through the Abyss, otherwise known as Daath or "Knowledge." Known as "The Uniting Intelligence" this pathway represents the journey of the Mystic pursuing the energy of the Heart through the lessons of the darkness to attain the Divine wisdom of the Crown. The Priestess is an appropriate card to govern this path as she represents Occult Wisdom, Esoteric Knowledge, secrets to be revealed, unfulfilled potential, and the feminine powers of intuition and Higher Understanding.

In examining the card of The High Priestess we are presented with a young woman seated between two pillars, one white and the other black. These pillars are of the mythical temple of Solomon the King and represent the basic opposing principles of the Universe. The black pillar bears the Hebrew letter Beth (B) and represents infinite potential and the white pillar bears the Hebrew letter Yod (J) and symbolizes the initiating force that acts upon potential. The hat worn by The Priestess is meant to symbolize the cycles of the Moon (the planet ruling the 13th Pathway) with the crescent shape on the left representing the waxing stage or the moon on her increase, the full circle in the center standing for both the New and Full Moons, and the crescent shape on the right symbolizing the waning stage or the moon on her decrease. In her lap The Priestess holds a scroll with the word "TORA" inscribed upon it. If an "H" is added to the word TORA one then has "TORAH" the Hebrew word for "The Law." With the final letter of this word covered by the Priestess's cape what we are presented with is a metaphor that is meant to imply that The Priestess represents the Secret Law (The Qabalah) that provides the true meaning behind the rhetorical Law. At the feet of The Priestess is the form of a crescent Moon, once again repeating the symbol for the ruling planetary aspect of this path. The designs of Palms and Pomegranates decorating the veil in the background are meant to symbolize the Lingam and Yoni of Tantric Mysticism and represent the male and female organs respectively, while the veil itself represents the mystery of death that has never been revealed. It should also be noted that the pomegranates depicted on the veil are arranged in the same order as the Spheres or "Sephirah" on the Tree of Life, thus insinuating that the secret beyond death is intimately linked with our connection to the Divine prototype within us that is represented by the Tree of Life.

THE EMPRESS.

© 1971 U.S. Games

The Empress signifies growth, fertility, potential fulfilled, happy, stable relationships, motherhood, and love. The planetary influence associated with this path is Venus and her symbol can be seen on a heart-shaped shield at the foot of The Empress's throne. A further examination of the card reveals golden stalks of corn growing abundantly all around The Empress with the golden color symbolizing the rays of the sun and the fruitful marriage of the heavens to the earth, a union further symbolized by the voluptuous green forest rising up in the background of the card. Also behind The Empress is a flowing stream that is supposed to be symbolic of the Life Force that exists within her, while on her gown are designs of Pomegranates that resemble the symbol for Venus, their combination alluding to both the Goddess energy and the Yoni of Tantric Mysticism. On top of the scepter held by The Empress is a globe that signifies the Earth and according to A.E. Waite "the card is a symbol of the door or gate by which an entrance is obtained into this life." In direct relation to this preceding point, the Hebrew letter associated with the card of The Empress through its mutual association with the 14th pathway on the Tree of Life is, Daleth (D), whose translation is "a door" and thus serves to literally support Mr. Waite's analogy of The Empress representing an entrance into earthly existence. That the principles of reproduction and regeneration embodied by The Empress are Higher Truths as well as earthly realities is illustrated by the cluster of a dozen six-pointed stars (signifying as above, so below) on her the crown, the number 12 further symbolizing the 12 Signs of the Zodiac. Because the card of The Empress is assigned to the 14th pathway on the Tree of Life that connects the Supernal Spheres of Chokmah and Binah, the essential Male and Female energies, this card can also be considered to represent the highest octave of human love and sexuality.

The meaning of The Emperor of the Tarot speaks to material success, stability, authority, ambition, and worldly achievement. It is the number IV card within the Major Arcana and the numerological significance of 4 is that of the square, the cube, the cross, and the four directions, all metaphors of the manifest world presided over by the energy of The Emperor. As an archetype, The Emperor represents executive realization as he sits on a throne made of interlocking four-sided slabs of stone that signify the stability and groundedness of the earth, a theme continued behind the throne in the rocky cliffs rising up in the background. Four Ram's heads decorate the back and armrests of the throne and this signifies the Astrological association with Aries, the Ram, the archetype representing the raw energy necessary to make things happen whose symbol is present on the top of the crown The Emperor is wearing. The red robe of The Emperor is the color associated with the element of Sulphur, the fiery, energetic principle of Earth heat in the transformational Spiritual Science of Alchemy. In his hands, The Emperor holds both a golden orb and a scepter that respectively symbolize his supreme rationality and male potency. Attributed to the 15th Pathway on the Tree of Life that extends down from the left side of the head on a forty-five degree diagonal over the collarbone and left breast to the center of the torso, The Emperor is one of a pair of Tarot Cards associated with the physical heart. Although the Sphere of Tiphareth on the Tree of Life is called the Heart Sphere, its actual placement on the body is in the center of the torso below where the actual organ of the heart would be. It is really the paths of The Emperor and The Hermit, the former passing over the left breast, that literally surround the position of the physical heart. This bit of information becomes quite ironic when one realizes that many of the qualities associated with The Emperor such as those of material success, ambition, and worldly achievement are also the cause of why so many adult males in contemporary American Society are over-stressed and suffering from cardio-vascular disease.

THE HIEROPHANT

© 1971 U.S. Games

Originally called "The Pope" in earlier decks, this card was re-titled "The Hierophant" by A.E. Waite in his rectified Tarot in order to intentionally move beyond the obvious dogma implied by the former name. The Hierophant was the title held by the Greek High Priest who presided over the Eleusinian Mysteries, and in choosing this descriptive Waite was intending the card to be more about a secret, inner tradition rather than exoteric doctrine. Ultimately though both approaches become the same, for in either case there is a prescribed code of conduct to be followed. Whether one joins a Mystery School or the Catholic Church there is still a tradition to be acknowledged. As a result,

The Hierophant is primarily a card of orthodoxy. While for some this function of Religion as merely a social institution is hypocritical and a waste of time, to the majority of people the tradition represented by The Hierophant makes them feel safe and secure. The true realm of the Spirit demands individual initiation and transformation, yet most people would rather not think about that and instead immerse themselves in the daily distractions of the material world. It therefore then becomes easier to let our Spiritual matters be handled by an industry of Professional Priests who seduce us into believing their manner and costumes represent true knowledge. This is exemplified in the image on the card by the colorful garb of The Hierophant and his Ministers that stands out in marked contrast to the colorless gray background of the temple. Even though the symbolism of the roses and lilies on the robes of the Ministers along with the crossed keys at the feet of The Hierophant do imply a balanced awareness of the mysteries of life and death, it is not necessarily important that the institution represented by these individuals actually offers any real answers concerning these matters. At the very least the orthodoxy implied by The Hierophant provides a place to begin for anyone who may truly be interested in pursuing a Spiritual Path.

The picture on the card of The Lovers depicts the Sun at its zenith, while in the sky just beneath the zenith, the Archangel Raphael bestows blessings upon a naked man and woman. Behind the figure of the woman is the Tree of Knowledge with a serpent entwined around it, and behind the man is The Tree of Life bearing its fruits. A closer examination of the image will further reveal that a triad is formed between the man, the woman, and the Angel with the man looking at the woman while she gazes at the Angel. This arrangement signifies that logic (represented by the man) cannot apprehend Spirit directly and it is only through uniting with the woman (symbolizing intuition) that Higher

Understanding can be attained.

A more mundane interpretation of The Lovers is that the card illustrates the most basic truth of the Universe, namely Love. The Physical, Spiritual, and Emotional joining between man and woman is the highest expression we are allowed in the human arena and the one brief respite we are furnished with as an alternative to the duality, longing, and suffering of this earthly life. In sexual union we are provided with the means to transcend our separateness and experience unity.

The card of The Lovers also speaks to our relationships in general and both the help we give or allow ourselves to receive from others. The Hebrew letter associated with this card is, Zayin (Z), meaning "a sword," which is a symbol associated with one of the four suits of the Tarot. The suit of Swords or "Knives" is governed by the element of air and relates to our mental processes as well as the adversity in our lives. The Astrological association for The Lovers is the Air Sign of Gemini or "The Twins" and it is in the social implications of this Sign along with the fact that Gemini is ruled by Mercury (the patron God of Magick) that points to The Lovers as revealing the esoteric challenges to being human and attempting to relate to others on a Higher Spiritual level.

© 1971 U.S. Games

The card of The Chariot is symbolic of overcoming obstacles, the power of self-assertion, and the triumph of the Higher Will, each of these meanings being further supported by the card's Astrological attribution of Cancer, the sign of the Zodiac marking the Summer Solstice or the Sun's extreme northern declination which represents the height of the growing season and the power of the Sun at its zenith. While on one level, The Chariot is a symbol of strength in adversity on the material plane, on another level it is also a Hermetic Alchemical reference to The Great Work. The psychologist Carl Jung pointed this out in his research when he drew an analogy between The Chariot of the Tarot and "The

Chariot of Antimony" mentioned in an Ancient Alchemical manuscript entitled "The Visions of Zosimos." In many Alchemical writings the element of Antimony was referred to as "The Lapis" or transformative Philosopher's Stone, and if one looks closely at the Tarot Card of The Chariot, the chariot itself seems to be made of a solid cube which looks remarkably like a piece of pure Antimony. The upper half of the Charioteer's body appears to be rising out of this solid, stone-like form, and if one thinks of the chariot as a cube of Antimony then the Charioteer can be viewed as the resurrected Spiritual man emerging from it. It is no surprise then when Israel Regardie affirms in his classic "A Garden of Pomegranates" that the card of The Chariot is symbolic of The Great Work.

In continuing to examine the imagery depicted in The Chariot, the reader will notice that a pair of Sphinxes, one white and one black, are harnessed to draw the chariot. These mythical animals are supposed to signify the opposing aspects of the Charioteer's nature that he must come to master in order to become the resurrected Spiritual man spoken of earlier. This inner conflict is additionally mirrored in the Chariot Driver's shoulder pads that depict a waxing and waning Moon, the waxing crescent harboring an angry face and the waning crescent containing a smiling face. On the front of the cart are another pair of symbols of The Great Work, the lower one in red signifying the joining of the Lingam and Yoni of Tantric Mysticism and the upper one showing a winged globe that symbolizes the Transcendental Self, or the wisdom needed to direct the energies of the Tantric Union toward their highest purpose. On the Charioteer's crown is an 8 pointed star representing Spiritual rebirth and attainment while on the canopy over the cart are the designs of stars, these being meant to represent the heavens or "Above," as opposed to the white square on the Charioteer's breastplate which is supposed to signify the material world or "Below."

The Sign of the Zodiac attributed to the card of Strength is Leo (the Lion), an association that seems quite appropriate because the image on the card portrays a maiden gently closing the mouth of a lion with her bare hands. The Maiden has an Infinity symbol above her head, which harkens back to the card of The Magician where the figure of The Mage also has an Infinity Symbol above his head. This common element in both cards speaks to the self-empowerment of the individual, with The Magician representing the initial thought, intention, or action necessary to manifest something and Strength referring to the courage, determination, and self-awareness needed for that initial intention to become a tangible result. The card of Strength is also a metaphor for taming the beast within, the lion in turn representing those lower aspects of human nature that each of us must master in order to manifest our highest potential. An important point to keep in mind while contemplating the card of Strength is that the fortitude implied is not necessarily brute force or rigid resistance. The power alluded to in Strength is often simply the capacity to maintain faith in the Higher purpose of our lives despite difficulties which at the moment may not seem to serve any other reason than to frighten or hurt us. An interesting anecdote relating to this is the belief by the Ancient Qabalistic Magicians that an Adept could literally walk into a lion's den without being harmed. This is possible because in order to be an Adept one needed to master and subsequently eliminate all fear, for it is our fear that infuriates the lion and causes the beast to lose its natural respect for a human being as a Higher form of existence.

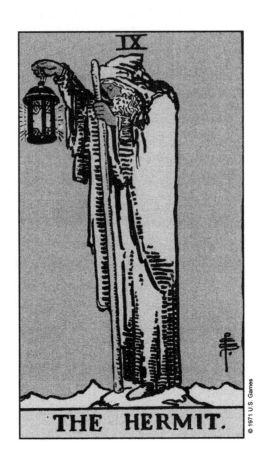

Depicting an elderly man in robes standing alone on a frozen mountaintop while holding a lantern, the card of The Hermit is symbolic of wisdom and Spiritual attainment. This interpretation becomes more obvious once it is noticed that the source of the light within the Hermit's lantern is in the shape of a 6 pointed star or "Hexagram," the symbol for the unification of the Heavens and the Earth. The letter of the Hebrew alphabet attributed to The Hermit is Yod (I) and the Astrological correspondence is Virgo or "The Virgin." To develop these associations a little further, the letter Yod would correspond to the paternal or initiating energy within the Tetragrammaton (IHVH) and Virgo would be analogous to the Egyptian Goddess Isis as the Divine Mother who is yet to be fertilized. If the Father energy of Yod is then associated with the heavens and the mother energy of Virgo is associated with the earth, we will once again find ourselves reflecting upon the same concept of above and below that is illustrated by the hexagram within The Hermit's lamp.

Beyond being symbolic of Spiritual attainment, the archetype of The Hermit is also about time and patience, for the elderly gentleman pictured in the card is the grown up version of the younger man in the card of The Magician. Where the young man in the number I Trump of the Major Arcana was focused on manipulating the outer environment illustrated by the 4 suits of the Tarot, the more experienced figure in The Hermit has learned that the material world is an illusion and the enlightened individual must create their own reality from within. The journey to such a mountaintop of understanding is a process that usually takes a lifetime, hence the age of The Hermit who shines as his own Sun in the desolation that routinely discourages and consumes those who have not evolved beyond their illusions.

WHEEL of FORTUNE.

© 1971 U.S. Games

On the spokes within the wheel that forms the central image in The Wheel of Fortune are the symbols for the 4 basic elements of Alchemy; Mercury (symbol), Sulphur (symbol), Water (symbol), and Salt (symbol). On the outer rim of the wheel at each of the cardinal points are the letters T, A, R, and O, which according to S.L. Mathers can be arranged to spell the following four words; ROTA (Wheel), TARO (Tarot), ORAT (Speaks), and TORA (The Law). These words can then be combined together to form the sentence "The Wheel of the Tarot speaks of the Law." Also on the outer rim of the Wheel at alternating positions between the letters T, A, R, and O are the 4 Hebrew letters Yod,

Heh, Vav, Heh or "IHVH," the ineffable name of God otherwise known as Tetragrammaton. As a result of all these various symbols that I have just pointed out, The Wheel is meant to signify the flow of the manifest world (or the Microcosm) as it is expressed by the 4 elements, the formula of Creation (IHVH), and the ability of human beings to master these phenomenon by consciously seeking out a Higher Wisdom (Tarot).

The images surrounding The Wheel speak of the heavenly realm or "The Macrocosm," beginning with the serpent to the left that symbolizes Transcendental Knowledge. The red figure to the right is the jackal-headed Egyptian God Anubis, the Divine escort for the souls of the dead to their final judgment, and the Blue Sphinx holding a sword that sits at the top of the wheel is a symbol of resurrection, the sword implying the ultimate victory of Spirit over the limitations of the flesh. In the four corners of the card are the four Fixed signs of the Zodiac; Aquarius (the Man reading), Scorpio (the Eagle), Taurus (the Bull), and Leo (the Lion). If a comparison is then made between these symbols of the Macrocosm and the symbols of the Microcosm that constituted the Wheel, the meaning of The Wheel of Fortune could be explained as "As Above, So Below" or the interconnectedness of all things through an eternal cycle of death and rebirth.

The image on the card of Justice is of a Queenly figure seated upon a throne. In her right hand this figure holds a sword that symbolizes power, while in her left hand she holds a set of scales that represent balance. Her cape is fastened upon her shoulders with a pin in the form of a red circle and upon her crown is a small blue square. The circle and the square represent celestial order and earthly order respectively, while the color red is significant of Alchemical Sulphur or "Earth Fire" and blue suggests the Heavenly realms. That the colors and shapes of these pins are matched to their opposites, specifically the circle of the heavens has the red of earth and the square of earth has the blue of the heavens, along with the fact that the circle is over the Queen's breast and the square is on her head, speaks to the necessity for the qualities usually associated with heart and mind, emotion and intellect, to be interchangeable if one hopes to truly attain the highest wisdom and balance signified by Justice.

The Mythological association for Justice is Athena, the Greek Goddess of War who, unlike Aries, her male counterpart, is about the use of strategy and intellect to attain victory rather than simple brute force. The Astrological association for Justice is the Sign of Libra, the sign of balance symbolized by the scales which are held by Lady Justice in her left hand. On a Magickal level, the meaning of the card of Justice speaks to the need to master and subsequently balance the extremes of our emotions and ego so that the oftentimes seemingly incomprehensible twists of fate illustrated in the previous card of The Wheel of Fortune may be accepted and ultimately turned to one's advantage.

THE HANGED MAN.

© 1971 U.S. Games

The Hanged Man is undoubtedly the most notorious card in the Tarot due to the paradoxical image it presents. In the card we see a young man hanging upside down on a T-shaped or "Tau" Cross. He is suspended by one leg tied at the ankle while his other leg is bent behind the first so that a cross is formed. Both of the young man's arms are behind his back, and if one looks closely at the way they are folded, it can be seen that a triangle is created with his shoulders as the base. Viewed as a whole, this positioning of his arms and legs form the shape of a cross over a triangle which was the symbol of the Hermetic Order of the Golden Dawn, a Magickal Society of which the Designer of the card (A.E. Waite) and the Illustrator (Pamela Coleman Smith) were members.

Despite the obviously uncomfortable looking position he is in, the young man in the card of The Hanged Man appears to be completely unruffled by his predicament. In fact, there is a glowing orb of light around his head that serves to give him a very enlightened and angelic appearance. The meaning of this card is commonly associated with obstacles and difficulty, although a higher interpretation behind its obvious facade would intimate transcendence over earthly limitations. The card of The Hanged Man can also imply an ultimate transcendence over the mystery of death. The regenerative aspect of the card's meaning is revealed by the fact that the T Cross from which the young man is suspended is a direct reference to the final letter of the Hebrew alphabet, Tav, thereby presenting the young man's glowing attitude as a metaphor of a Higher awareness beyond what is thought to be the end, or death. The fact that the Cross is also sprouting leaves despite its having been felled is a further hint at the existence of a new life beyond death. The Hebrew letter attributed to the card of The Hanged Man is Mem (M), the 13th letter of the Hebrew alphabet which translates as "Water." This is significant in that water is symbolic of the emotions and the mystery within the card of The Hanged Man is clearly expressed through the lack of emotion on the part of the hanging young man, emotions of course often representing those attempts on the part of our lower ego to hold us back from evolving to a higher, balanced awareness.

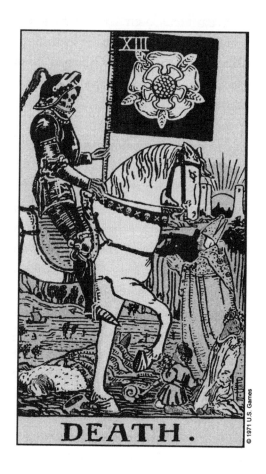

The biggest obstacle we face as human beings and the greatest mystery our intelligence has to ponder is the basic fact of death. All fear, and I dare say, all religion is a reaction to this unavoidable phenomenon. As a result, any image associated with death will be sure to evoke both fear and anxiety in many people. It is therefore necessary that the Tarot, or any other system of higher symbolism, include some form of reckoning with death for the act of dying represents the most important thing to understand on the path to enlightenment; specifically that the only constant and permanent thing in the universe is change.

Looking at the card of Death, the prominent image is that of a yellow skeleton in black armor mounted on a white horse. In its hand, the skeleton is holding a black banner adorned with a white flower that is supposed to represent the rose of life. The figure of Death is riding forward on his steed and as he goes he is confronted by an array of figures; a priest in prayer, a maiden looking away, a man lying face up, and a small child, yet it is only the child who seems at ease as Death approaches, for in their openness and naivete, children possess the appropriate attitude to be able to flow with change and not get caught up in denial and fear. The river in the background is meant to symbolize the River Styx of Greek Mythology that leads to the Kingdom of the Dead or "Hades," (the blue tinted landscape comprising the background of the card) while the Sun rising between a pair of pillars in the distance beyond the blue landscape speaks of Death as a transition between states of being rather than an absolute end.

In "A Garden of Pomegranates," Israel Regardie writes that the Magickal Formula associated with this card is "regeneration through putrefication" referring to a step in the Ancient Science of Alchemy which attempted to transmute base metals into gold through a process of chemical and esoteric alterations. The direction of these alterations followed first a process of descent known as "The Nigredo" (which is analogous to the black armor worn by the mounted skeleton) where the common properties of the base metals involved were broken down and destroyed, and then a process of ascent whereby with the addition of certain other ingredients the essential spirit of gold within the base matter (represented by the skeleton's yellow color) could be identified and then extracted. This procedure was named, "The Stairway of Planets" by the Ancient Alchemists and referred not only to the material transformation of the elements involved, but also to the inner transformation of the Alchemist as well. Below is a table illustrating the 7 steps in the Stairway of Planets.

PLANET	METAL
Mercury	Quicksilver
Venus	Copper
Mars	Iron
Jupiter	Tin
Saturn	Lead
Moon	Silver
Sun	Gold

As a result of this analogy to Classical Alchemy, I would hope the reader has noticed that as we have gone along, the Tarot has also exhibited its own version of The Stairway of Planets. The cards that have been covered thus far have led us to a symbolic descent (represented by this current section on Death) and the upcoming cards will eventually progress to a symbolic apex (the card of The Sun XIX) which would be synonymous with the fabled Divine Gold of Alchemy.

The Angel in the card of Temperance is wearing a headpiece adorned with the Astrological symbol of the Sun, implying enlightenment from Higher sources, while on the front of his white robe there is a golden triangle pointing upwards that represents aspiration. This triangle is in turn contained within a square, symbolizing material reality, and above this square are the 4 Hebrew letters that spell Tetragrammaton (IHVH) or the Magickal formula for creation. In each of his hands the Angel is holding a chalice, one silver and one gold, while pouring water back and forth between them. This action symbolizes the flow between the subconscious and conscious mind, for in Alchemy silver represents the Moon, or the subconscious, and gold represents the Sun or the conscious mind. The act of pouring also speaks to the necessity for our emotions to be always flowing, for when water is left to stand it becomes a breeding ground for parasitic organisms and the same will occur if we allow our emotions to remain stagnant. This insight is reinforced when one notices that the Angel has one foot in the water and the other on dry land, the water representing the subconscious and the earth signifying the conscious mind. On the left side of the picture a path leads from the pool of water to a distant mountaintop upon which there shines a brilliant light. Within the aura of this light the outline of a crown can be detected which is intended to show that the balance of our conscious and subconscious awareness as portrayed within the image of Temperance is what constitutes the true path to Higher Consciousness. The Astrological attribution for this card is Sagittarius, the sign symbolizing Spiritual aspiration and Higher Enlightenment. The pair of irises flowering among the reeds in the lower right hand corner of the card are symbolic of the Greek Goddess Iris, ruler of the rainbow and the personal messenger of the ruling couple of Mount Olympus, Zeus and Hera. Because of her courtesy and amiable demeanor, Iris was beloved by both Gods and humans alike and the flowers named in her honor signify that the connection between the heavens and the earth is an open and loving one for whoever strives to embody the proper temperance of Spirit.

THE DEVIL .

© 1971 U.S. Games

Portrayed as a half-man, half-goat creature with horns, the image of The Devil in this card is derived from the Greek God Pan, otherwise known as the Shepherd's God, who was worshiped as a life giving fertility figure that represented untamed nature and sexuality. With the rise of Christianity in Medieval times and that religion's need to repress and control the minds of its followers, this sort of archetypal image was considered evil and subsequently banished by the dogma of the Church to represent the lower realms. On the top of The Devil's head is an upside down 5 pointed star or "Pentagram," a symbol spoken of in an earlier chapter when it was explained that an upright Pentagram represents the dominance of Spirit (symbolized by the top point of the star) over the 4 basic elements of the material world (air, fire, earth, and water symbolized by the 4 lower points of the star). The reversed Pentagram on The Devil's head would then imply that the desires of our material or lower nature have taken precedence over the higher, more balanced qualities of our humanity that allow us to feel compassion and concern beyond individual ego. In addition, by the way the reversed Pentagram is imposed upon the head of The Devil we are able to see how the reversed star resembles the actual head of a goat with the horns, ears, and jaw. Standing beneath The Devil are the naked figures of a man and a woman, both of who are chained by the neck to the foundation on which The Devil is perched. Upon examining the figures, it becomes plain that the shackles around their necks are loose enough so as to be easily lifted off, intimating that it is more our own weakness or the unwillingness to change a situation that empowers The Devil rather than our being the victims of any dark force or evil entity beyond our mettle. In regards to one's personal development, the card of The Devil represents blockages within us that prevent the exercising of our Higher nature as well as an excessive attachment to ego and the material world with its obsessions and desires. The Astrological association for the card of the The Devil is the sign of Capricorn (the Goat) and in the raised hand of The Demon the symbol for the planet Saturn (the ruler of Capricorn) is visible in his palm. The Hebrew letter assigned to this card is, Ayin (O), which translates as "an Eye."

THE TOWER.

© 1971 U.S. Games

The image in this card shows a tower on a cliff being struck by a zig-zag bolt of lightning while at the same time the top of the tower, depicted as a crown, is being blown off. The lightning bolt is significant of Higher Consciousness and the exploding crown speaks to the enlightenment resulting from the dismantling of a house of falsehood and the dissolution of thought patterns that create rigid and limiting structures in our lives. As a result, The Tower refers to the need to eliminate false philosophies and rebuild in their place new ways of understanding life.

For many people, The Tower is a frightening card because it is often about upsetting the things in our lives we habitually look to for stability. A perfect illustration of this concept materialized to a shocking degree with the terrorist attacks on the World Trade Center on September 11, 2001. The horror of planes intentionally crashing into the Twin Towers was more than an attack on a specific place in time, it was also an assault on the collective consciousness of a people who assumed themselves to be insulated from such occurrences because of what eventually proved to be a false sense of security. In the aftermath of this tragedy, the most important issue should not be merely revenge, or even rebuilding just for the sake of replacing the same idea with a different facade. The deeper meaning of this situation as per the criteria of The Tower speaks to questioning what The Twin Towers represented to the world and why would the business going on there make it a target for terrorists trying to make a point? It is too facile a conclusion to merely demonize the perpetrators as evil lunatics. To not address possible deeper issues of our own culpability is to run the risk that whatever is rebuilt on the site of the Twin Towers might very well end up being established upon a foundation of illusion that could possibly manifest a repeat of the same tragic conclusion.

After the previous Trump cards of The Devil and The Tower, The Star represents a rejuvenation or rebirth following a symbolic descent. The black background and somber feel of The Devil and The Tower are intentional, the black mirroring the Alchemical descent into "The Nigredo" or lowest point to which the soul must go before it can begin its rise toward the light. The depths of the Nigredo are symbolized by the element of lead, with The Star representing a release of that weight and density. This stage of release was referred to by the Alchemists as "The Albedo" or whitening, and symbolizes the transition from base lead to silver in The Stairway of Planets. This process included two steps: first the heating, which turned the lead white, and then the dissolution, a watery process designed to leach out the impurities within the bleached lead. Where the Nigredo stood for a symbolic Spiritual death, the Albedo was representational of the moment of baptism or rebirth. This sense of rejuvenation is illustrated in the card of The Star by the form of a naked maiden holding a pitcher in each of her hands and pouring water into a small pool as well as onto the dry land. The maiden symbolizes purity and the water is significant of our emotions. The act of the figure pouring water represents a replenishment of both the subconscious mind (the pool) and the conscious mind (the land) with a newfound optimism and energy, while the 5 small streams that have been created by the water poured upon the land are intended to represent the 5 senses. In the sky above the maiden is a large, golden 8-pointed star that is in turn surrounded by 7 smaller 8 pointed stars, the number 8 being the numerical symbol of baptism in Medieval times. The Astrological sign associated with The Star is Aquarius as a result of the similarities between the maiden depicted pouring water in the card and the Greek Mythological character of Ganymede, the beautiful youth who acted as the water bearer for the Gods on Mount Olympus.

After the bright environment of The Star, The Moon is a midnight landscape, a shadowy netherworld that speaks to an evolving consciousness not yet fully attained. At the top of the card is an image of an eclipse with the Moon conjunct over the Sun. In Alchemy this marriage of the Sun and the Moon is known as "Hierosgamos" and refers to the active masculine principle being able to regenerate by immersing itself into the body of its feminine opposite. Just below the eclipse, on opposite sides of the image, are two towers in the distance that are meant to symbolize the polarities of the conscious and unconscious mind. The realm of The Moon is the doorway between these two states and would correspond to the dimension of dreams or "The Astral Plane." In the middle ground of the image are a pair of canines baying at the Moon, one being a wolf and symbolizing the soul and the other being a dog and symbolizing the spirit. The dominant colors of the card are also significant in that white, blue, and yellow represent respectively the elements of salt, quicksilver, and gold in Alchemy. Salt symbolizes the passive material element, quicksilver the active Spiritual force, and gold the enlightenment resulting from the interaction of the first two. In addition, the heavenly body of the Moon was greatly revered by the Ancient Alchemists because it existed on the border between the light and the darkness and was mutable to either environment like Mercurius (Mercury), the patron God of Alchemy and the lone being that could traverse all the various dimensions of consciousness with impunity. At the bottom of the card is a small pool out of which a crustacean scuttles up on to the land. The pool is representative of both memory and the subconscious with the creature crawling out of the depths signifying our worst archetypal fears that must be overcome if we are to follow the winding road within the card that disappears into the distance of our inner landscape. The crustacean in the card may also signify a crab, thus drawing an association to the Astrological sign of Cancer where the Moon is the ruling planet. Additional meanings associated with the card of The Moon are fluctuation, change, uncertainty, and illusion, as well as finding solutions to our problems within the world of dreams and intuition rather than through logic or reason.

In the Alchemical process known as "The Stairway of Planets" the planetary sphere of the Sun represents the highest step on the ladder of ascension, namely the transmuted Gold of the Spirit. In the illustration on the Tarot card of The Sun, this form of exalted consciousness is symbolized by a joyful, naked child holding a red banner and riding triumphantly on a white horse. The white color of the horse is symbolic of the element of salt, or the earth, and the red banner represents the element of Sulphur, or the catalytic action necessary for the potential of the earth to give birth to new life symbolized by the child. Within the Major Arcana, the card of The Sun marks The Fool's ascension into the light after the trials of the underworld and represents a celebration of the journey through the archetypes of the Universal Self. The Hebrew letter associated with this card is Resh, which translates as "The Head" and the assigned pathway on the Tree of Life is the 30th, otherwise known as "The Collecting Intelligence." The Mythological figures associated with this path are Apollo, the Greek God of the Sun, and Ra, the Egyptian God of the Sun. The animal association is the Lion and the Astrological association is Leo, the sign of the Zodiac ruled by the Sun. The various other meanings associated with the card of The Sun are joy, prosperity, happiness, and true friendship.

After the symbolic enlightenment of The Sun we come next to the card of Judgment, the twenty-first of the twenty-two cards within the Major Arcana. Significant of a final reckoning as well as attained liberation, Judgment stands for the release from the confines of any previous limitation. The image on the card presents the Archangel Gabriel blowing his trumpet in the heavens, while below him the bodies of the dead rise from caskets that bob on the waves of the ocean like a flotilla of small boats. The sea is symbolic of the Great Collective Unconscious of Humanity and the golden hair of the Archangel along with his golden trumpet are both metaphorical of the Divine gold of the

Spirit that flows from heaven. The reader should notice that the three resurrected figures in the foreground also have golden hair signifying that they have received the heavenly Spirit from the Angel and therefore redemption for their souls. Also significant is that these three figures form a triad of Father, Mother, and Child, mirroring the Supernal Triad of the first three Spheres of The Tree of Life or the new consciousness born from the union of duality. Attached to the Archangel's horn is a white banner emblazoned with a red cross that is meant to be symbolic of the "Chemical Wedding" or the metaphorical marriage of the Sun and the Moon in Alchemy that represents both transcendence and enlightenment. Other meanings associated with the card of Judgment speak to starting with a clean slate after paying necessary debts, resurrection, rewards for past efforts, renewal, and rejuvenation.

The central image in the card of The World depicts what appears to be a dancing naked woman who has a purple sash covering her genitals. In each of her hands this figure holds a wand of the same sort held by the character in the card of The Magician. This Dancer is in turn positioned inside a large laurel wreath that has red bands wound in figure eights around its top and bottom. Outside of the perimeter of the wreath, in the four corners of the card, are representations of each of the four fixed signs of the Zodiac.

Initially, one would assume that the figure depicted in The World is a young woman simply because her naked breasts are revealed, however, upon a closer examination of the symbolism within the card the sexual persuasion of this figure is not really so clear-cut. In the other cards of the Major Arcana that include naked female figures such as The Lovers, The Devil, and The Star, the illustrator of the deck did not feel modesty was necessary and the women depicted in those cards are entirely naked with their genitals exposed. Could it then be intentional that the reproductive organs of the dancer in The World are covered because the sex of the figure is supposed to be ambiguous? The wands held by the figure in The World are the same style as the wand held by the Mage in the card of The Magician, except the Mage has only one wand while the figure in The World holds a pair of wands. The single wand held by The Magician represents the initiating act of creation therefore making the intention behind the card comparable to the masculine sexual energy. With this in mind, the two wands held by the figure in The World could then be viewed as signifying a dual sexual energy or both the male and female aspects necessary for creation. The apparent androgyny of this figure, along with the knowledge that the card of The World is assigned to the final pathway on the Tree of Life, could then be seen as a metaphor of the Divine state of Unity available to those who have passed the process of Initiation illustrated in the Major Arcana.

The laurel wreath surrounding the figure in The World is supposed to represent the "Vesica Pisces" of Sacred Geometry, or the symbolic doorway through which a third shape is born from the interpenetration of two spheres. It makes perfect sense for the Dancer to be contained within such a symbolic area as the positioning serves to reinforce the concept of the figure in The World being an androgynous representation of Unity. The red sashes in the forms of figure eights or "Infinity Symbols" wound around both the top and bottom of the wreath signify through their color the catalytic element of Sulphur in alchemy and by their shape the eternal process of creation which is facilitated by the energy of Sulphur. The images corresponding to the four Fixed

Signs of the Zodiac (Aquarius, Scorpio, Taurus, and Leo) located in the four corners of the card are further meant to signify the four earthly elements of Air, Water, Earth, and Fire respectively and hence also illustrate the union of the heavens and earth, or the completion of the Great Work as it is expressed in the Major Arcana of the Tarot.

❖❖❖

CHAPTER V

THE
PYTHAGOREAN CROSS

HE premise behind the Science of Sacred Geometry is that the universe consists of an infinite number of perfectly proportioned relationships between certain basic forms. The perfect interlocking of these basic forms is referred to as "embedding" and operates on the same general premise as a jigsaw puzzle except that in Sacred Geometry, the individual parts which comprise the whole must be regular and perfect in their own rite, quite unlike the pieces in a jigsaw puzzle. The characteristic that will allow a shape to embed and perpetuate itself eternally, either through expansion or reduction, is that the shape's proportions are in the Phi ratio or "Golden Mean" established by the Ancient Greek Philosopher Pythagoras.

The simplest way of explaining the Phi ratio is to draw a line and divide it into two sections;

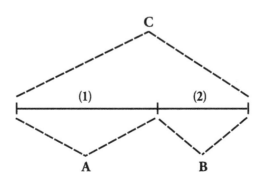

Illus. 14

The ratio of the entire line (C) to the larger segment (A) is exactly the same as the ratio of the larger segment (A) to the smaller section (B). The number which defines this ratio is a never ending decimal which computed up to six digits is, 1.61803....

In order to see how this line can embed infinitely, one simply needs to fold over the smaller section into the larger one, thereby recreating a smaller version of the entire line (C). This process can then be repeated over and over forever without ever running out of a line to divide.

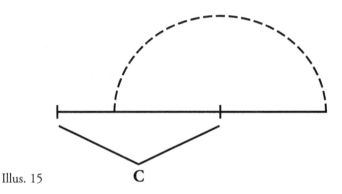

Illus. 15   C

The Golden Mean of Pythagoras was later applied to Nature by an Italian mathematician named Leonardo of Pisa (1180-1250) better known as "Fibonacci." When he started to observe certain patterns in nature, such as how flowering plants reproduce, Fibonacci discovered some very exciting and enlightening information. From this data he constructed a number pattern known as "The Fibonacci Series" in which each number after the first is arrived at by adding together the two numbers that precede it. For example, 0+1=1, 1+1=2, 1+2=3, 2+3=5, etc. which results in the following pattern;

0, 1, 1, 2, 3, 5, 8, 13, 21, 34, 55, 89, 144......

If any number in the Fibonacci Series is divided by the number that immediately precedes it (for instance 13 divided by

8) the answer will get progressively closer to 1.618… as the size of the numbers increase, which essentially creates the perfect algorhythm for growth.

The concept of embedding also applies to a Pythagorean right triangle whose sides are in the proportion of 3, 4, and 5. This can be illustrated by making a rectangle of adjoining 3, 4, 5 Pythagorean triangles and then further dividing this area into proportionately smaller and smaller rectangles and triangles so that an infinitely embedded pattern is created.

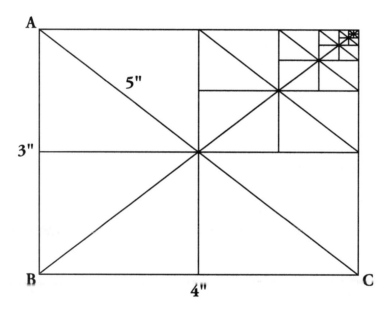

Illus. 16

The characteristic of being able to embed infinitely is the first of two reasons why I chose the Pythagorean Right Triangle as the basis to design a reference key for the three interlocking symbolic languages of Western Esotericism (Qabalah, Astrology, and Tarot).

The second reason is that for the Hermetic/Rosicrucian Philosopher, a Pythagorean Right Triangle in the proportion of 3, 4, 5, presents a diagram that succinctly summarizes the Great Work. To create this diagram one would begin by assigning the

Egyptian God Osiris (the Father) to the side of the triangle measuring 3, the Goddess Isis (the Mother) to the side measuring 4, and the Child Horus to the hypotenuse which measures 5.

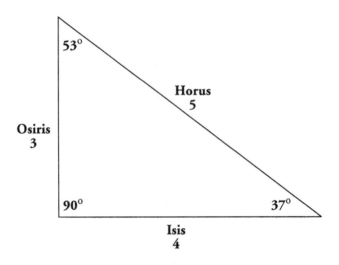

The largest angle of the triangle measures 90 degrees and joins the lines of Osiris and Isis (Father and Mother). The number 90 represents the Astrological aspect of a Square or the aspect of "Manifestation." In Hebrew a word with the numerical value of 90 is IKIN or "Jachin" one of the two great pillars of the Temple of Solomon the King that represents the male or initiating principle of creation. The angle joining the lines of Isis and Horus (Mother and Son) measures 37 degrees, 37 being the value of the Hebrew name HBL or "Abel" the second son of Adam in the Bible who was slain by his brother Cain. In Christian Theology it is commonly understood that Abel represents an early prototype of Christ, who was in turn based somewhat on the earlier prototype of Horus of the Egyptians. The final angle of the triangle joining the sides attributed to the Child Horus and the Father Osiris measures 53 degrees, the numerical value for the Hebrew word ABN or "Stone." For the Qabalist, this word intimates the Philosopher's Stone of Alchemy because it represents the union of the Father (AB in Hebrew) and the Son (BN in Hebrew) or the Mystical union of the Consciousness of the One Infinite Creator with that of individual human awareness.

The Key I have subsequently designed using this sacred triangular shape has been constructed in the form of a cross and consists of 32 Pythagorean Right Triangles corresponding to the 10 Spheres and 22 connecting Pathways of the Tree of Life (See diagram at the end of this chapter).

In the pair of reference keys for the diagram, it can be seen that the 22 triangles comprising the vertical column of the Cross represent the Pathways of the Tree, while the two arms, each consisting of 5 triangles, correspond to the Spheres. The angles of each individual triangle then in turn contain the Hebrew letter (or Sphere name), Astrological (or elemental) correspondence, and Tarot attribution for each Sphere or Pathway. The reader can readily see for instance that triangle 25 refers to the 25th Pathway on the Tree of Life, which is attributed the Hebrew letter Samekh (**S**) with a numerical value of 60, the Astrological sign of Sagittarius ♐, and the Tarot Trump of Temperance XIV.

I originally designed this table for myself so that I wouldn't have to continually flip back and forth through reference books when either studying or writing, and in very little time found that I was able to retain the information so that I no longer needed the table. The importance of this Pythagorean Cross as a study guide should therefore not be underestimated because one of the basic keys to understanding and using the languages of Western Esotericism effectively is to realize how all three of these languages are interactive parts of a unified whole.

Due to the obvious limit of space within each individual triangle of the Cross, it was not possible to write out all the information fully. As a result, I have used the abbreviated Hebrew spellings for the Spheres and the traditional symbols for the Planets, Elements, and Signs of the Zodiac.

Sephiroth

KThR - Kether   ChSD- Chesed   NTzCh - Netzach

ChKMH - Chokmah   GBVRH - Geburah   HVD - Hod

BINH - Binah   ThPARTh - Tiphareth   YSVD - Yesod

                       MLKVTh - Malkuth

Elements

△ Fire   △ Air   ▽ Water   ▽ Earth

Planets

♄ Saturn   ♆ Neptune   ♀ Venus   ♂ Mars

☉ Sun   ☽ Moon   ☿ Mercury ⊕ Earth

♃ Jupiter

Zodiac

♈ Aries   ♌ Leo   ♐ Sagittarius

♉ Taurus   ♍ Virgo   ♑ Capricorn

♊ Gemini   ♎ Libra   ♒ Aquarius

♋ Cancer   ♏ Scorpio   ♓ Pisces

Illus. 18

In addition, I have chosen to use the English translations of the Hebrew letters in this key so that it would be more easily comprehensible to an English speaking audience, Following is a table of the Hebrew alphabet from the chapter on the Qabalah which includes these translations.

❖❖❖

HEBREW ALPHABET

Hebrew Letter	Numerical Value	Hebrew Letter Name	Signification of Name	Roman Letter
א	1	Aleph	Ox, also Duke, or Leader	A
ב	2	Beth	House	B
ג	3	Gimel	Camel	G
ד	4	Daleth	Door	D
ה	5	He	Window	H
ו	6	Vau	Peg, Nail	V
ז	7	Zayin	Weapon, Sword	Z
ח	8	Cheth	Enclosure, Fence	Ch
ט	9	Teth	Serpent	T
י	10	Yod	Hand	I
כ Final = ך	20 Final = 500	Kaph	Palm of the hand	K
ל	30	lamed	Ox-Goad	L
מ Final = ם	40 Final = 600	Mem	Water	M
נ Final = ן	50 Final = 700	Nun	Fish	N
ס	60	Samekh	Prop, Support	S
ע	70	Ayin	Eye	O
פ Final = ף	80 Final = 800	Pe	Mouth	P
צ Final = ץ	90 Final = 900	Tzaddi	Fishing-hook	Tz
ק	100	Qoph	Back of the head	Q
ר	200	Resh	Head	R
ש	300	Shin	Tooth	S, Sh
ת	400	Tau	Sign of the Cross	T, Th

Illus. 19

PYTHAGOREAN CROSS
OF THE MYSTERY SCIENCES

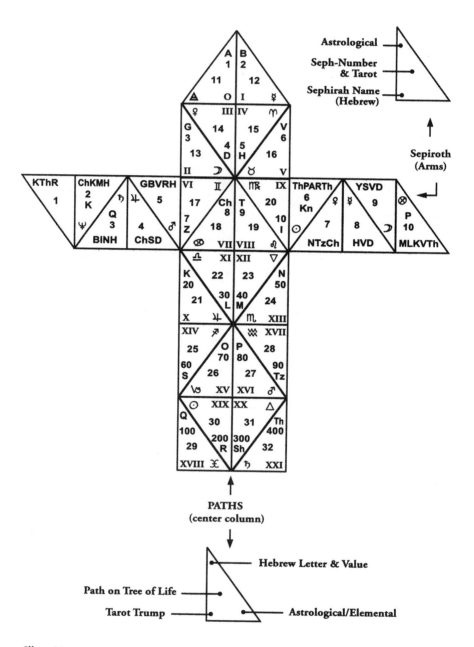

Illus. 20

PART II

MAGICKAL FORMS

CHAPTER VI

SACRED SHAPES

HE first four chapters of this book outline the basic principles of the three branches that constitute the language of Ritual Magick (Qabalah, Astrology, and Tarot). In the fifth chapter the reader was presented with a reference table entitled "The Pythagorean Cross" which illustrated the interworkings of these various branches of Magickal Language. Now that a diverse and interactive symbolic vocabulary is at our disposal, the next step will be to explore some formal strategies for the use of this symbolism.

The strategies to which I am referring consist of utilizing the three languages of Magick within palettes of Sacred Shape to create Talismans. By the term Sacred Shapes I mean the perfect Geometric Forms whose proportions serve as mathematical explanations of our perceptual reality. It was mentioned in the chapter on Astrology that Venus is the planet which governs Occult Knowledge; as a result of this association I have subsequently decided to focus on the number attributed to this archetype and discuss 7 basic Sacred Shapes: the Circle, the Triangle, the Square, the Pentagram, the Hexagram, the Heptagram, and the Cross.

THE CIRCLE

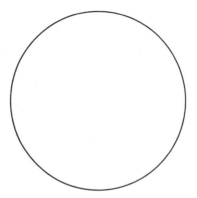

Illus. 21

The Circle symbolizes the Universe, or the unity of all things. It is also a symbol of balance since all the points on the circumference of a circle are equidistant from the center. In addition, the circle represents the cycles of the natural world and the perpetual flow of life into death, and death into rebirth. For the Magician, the circle represents the nature of the Great Work through its connections to unity, balance, and focus, the last of these aspects deriving from the fact that in all Ritual Workings the Magician creates a circle around himself as a vortex both for protection and invocation.

THE TRIANGLE

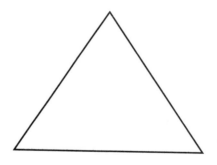

Illus. 22

The Greek Philosopher Pythagoras believed that the triangle was the basic building block of all reality. By elevating this particular shape to such a lofty theoretical position he was also simultaneously supporting its Occult meaning of pointing toward Higher Spiritual Truths. An example of the Occult meaning of the triangle is expressed by the Supernal Triad of the Tree of Life where Unity, represented by the first sphere of Kether, defines itself through an extension into basic duality, expressed as the second and third spheres of Chokmah and Binah (the primordial male and female energies). Pythagoras arrived at his theory on the triangle as a result of his explorations into musical harmony. In his research, Pythagoras noticed that all musical tones corresponded to simple ratios of numbers and these relationships in turn involved only the values of 1, 2, 3, and 4, along with their combined total of 10. To illustrate these relationships, Pythagoras designed a triangle consisting of 10 dots divided into 4 lines that he named "Tetraktys."

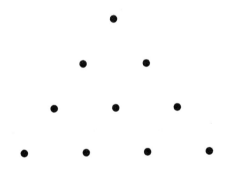

Illus. 23

As a pure mathematical construction, the triangle formed by the Tetraktys is also a diagram that explains the three dimensions of earthly reality. The single dot at the apex represents the lone point in space (•), while the pair of dots on the second level can be utilized to form a line (•——•), or the basic connection between separate points. The third level of three dots symbolizes the corners of a triangle and introduces surface (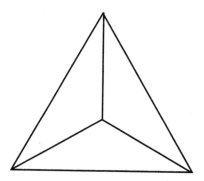), while the fourth level of four dots takes the previously created triangular surface and adds depth to produce a third dimension in the form of a four sided pyramid called, "A Tetrahedron."

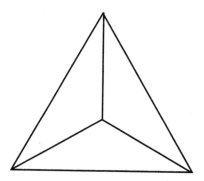

Illus. 24

The astute reader will no doubt notice that this theory of Tetraktys is essentially a more abstract restating of the concept of Tetragrammaton (the Qabalistic theory of Creation) explained in the chapter on the Tarot whereby four basic units merge to create an infinite algorhythm for growth.

THE SQUARE

Illus. 25

The Square represents the material world of the four elements (fire, water, air, and earth) and the four directions (north, south, east, and west). Because of its four equal sides and four equal angles, the Square is also a symbol of stability and balance. If one were to divide a square equally into four smaller squares and then place two of the Hebrew names for God, AHIH (Existence) and IHVH (Creation), within these four sub-squares, the result would be a perfect acrostic that could be read either vertically or horizontally to illustrate the perfect coalescence of existence and creation within the manifest world.

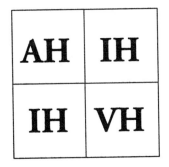

Illus. 26

THE PENTAGRAM

Illus. 27

The Magickal significance of the Pentagram was discussed in Chapter II with the description of a Qabalistic operation known as "Squaring the Circle." The Pentagram was also a shape that fascinated Pythagoras, in fact a 5 pointed star surrounded by a Pentagon was the special symbol of the order formed by his disciples.

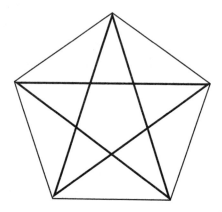

Illus. 28

Upon examining this symbol, it can be seen that the diagonal lines which form the 5 pointed star intersect in such a way that they end up forming a smaller, reversed pentagon within the center of the star. If the diagonals of this smaller pentagon are then drawn, the result will be yet another star containing a pentagon, and so on to infinity.

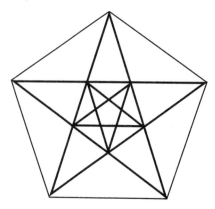

Illus. 29

The ratios of the various diagonals within these interlocking shapes that facilitate the phenomenon of the five pointed star being able to regenerate itself to infinity is an example of the "Golden Mean" and the subsequent concept of "Embedding" explained earlier in Chapter V.

An additional point of Magickal significance regarding the Pentagram is that the Divine name associated with this shape is, YHShVH or "Jeheshuah" (Jesus in English) which represents Spirit (the letter Shin) implanted within the formula for Creation (IHVH), or the essence of God that exists within the form of every human being. The letter Shin is associated with Spirit in this case because the numerical value of this Hebrew letter is 300 and the total of the expression, RVCh ALHIM (Ruach Elohim) or "The breath of the One in the Many" (the Holy Spirit of Catholicism) is also 300. The Pentagram is also a symbol for the beginning of The Great Work in Ritual Magick because the actual form of the star itself resembles the human form reaching for union with the aspect of Spirit assigned to the top point of the Pentagram.

THE HEXAGRAM

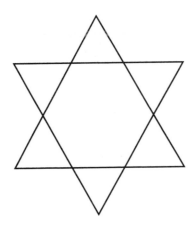

Illus. 30

The 6 pointed star or "Hexagram" symbolizes the concept of "As Above, So Below" because the interlocking, equilateral triangles that constitute the star can be thought of as representing the earth and the heavens, or the material ego of each human being as opposed to his or her Higher, Divine Genius. This idea of the unification of the Divine with the earthly makes the hexagram the symbol for the completion of the Great Work in Ritual Magick when it is compared to the Pentagram and the reaching toward spirit that the 5 pointed star symbolizes. The Magickal word associated with the Hexagram is "ARARITA" a notariqon (acronym) discussed in Chapter II which translates as "One is his beginning; One is his individuality; his permutation is One."

THE HEPTAGRAM

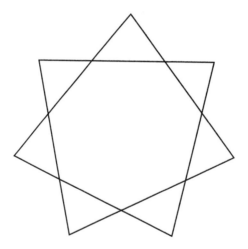

Illus. 31

The 7 pointed star or "Heptagram" (also known as the "Star of Venus" because its seven points correspond to the Qabalistic number for that planet) is a figure within which there exists a plethora of esoteric knowledge. The mysteries of the Heptagram are largely revealed in the "Fama Fraternitatis" of the Order of the Rosicrucians, a manifesto that first appeared in printed form in

Germany around 1610. The mythical founder of this Order, Brother Christian Rosenkreutz, was believed to have been secretly buried in a seven-sided vault that was not discovered until 120 years after his death. An analysis of this chamber based on examining the ratios of its sides and angles reveals a complex and illuminating set of correspondences that are a brilliant synthesis of the philosophies of both the Qabalah and Gnostic Christianity.

One example of the esoteric correspondences associated with the vault concerns the 120 years that elapsed before the discovery of the entombed Brother C. The number 120 refers to "The Magickal Age," whereby an individual has gained full insight into the mysteries of the Occult. Since each person must rediscover this symbolic vault on their own, the chamber is only accessible to those who have achieved this level of Magickal maturity. For a further explanation of what this maturity entails, I will utilize the Qabalistic technique of Gematria to uncover the esoteric correspondences to the number 120.

There are three Hebrew words having a numerical total of 120 which serve our purposes and they are KOL or "Master", SMK or "Samekh", the full spelling of the 15th letter of the Hebrew alphabet whose Tarot correspondence is Temperance XIV which symbolizes balance, and ON, a name of God. From these three words one may then ascertain "Only the Mastery of Inner Balance will reveal God."

Another example of the mysteries concealed within the vault concerns its seven sides, each of which is described as a rectangle measuring five by eight feet. This would result in the total perimeter length of any one side being 26, the Gematria of IHVH or "Jehovah." From this, one may interpret that whoever stands in the vault is faced by God on every side.

It was mentioned at the beginning of this section that the mysteries of the heptagram as the vault of Brother C are numerous; however, it is not the purpose of this book to fully explore a document as erudite as "The Fama Fraternitatis." Instead, for the sake of this manuscript's humble intentions, let's finish up this section by taking a brief look at the heptagram from a Pythagorean perspective.

In the following diagram, the same type of embedded pattern that was illustrated in the Pentagram/Pentagon emblem of the Pythagoreans is also evident if one places a Heptagram (7 pointed star) within a Heptagon (a simple 7 sided figure). A noteworthy addition in the following diagram is that the illustration includes two overlapping forms of the 7 pointed star, one with sharper points and one with broader points, thus the ensuing embedded pattern produces its inner Heptagon from the marriage of two stars.

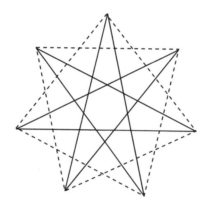

Illus. 32

A deeper aspect of this Star Marriage will be revealed if once again the Qabalistic practice of Gematria is used as it was in the analysis of the vault. Since the Heptagram is "The Star of Venus" let us first compute the numerical value of Venus or "NVGH" in Hebrew. The breakdown would be, N=50, V=6, G=3, H=5, thus NVGH = 64. The number 64 also represents the sum of the Hebrew words for Adam (ADM, which equals 45) and Eve (ChVH, which equals 19). Thus in the two inter-locking forms of The Star of Venus (named after the Goddess of Love) a metaphorical relationship is expressed that mirrors the basic energy of creation that is governed by Venus (Adam + Eve or male + female).

THE CROSS

Illus. 33

The most familiar form of the cross to many people is the Christian Cross upon which Jesus Christ was murdered. For centuries this symbol has been used to express the suffering of the spiritual path, yet in this section I will attempt to go beyond this dogma to reveal what is actually a very potent Magickal symbol.

In contrast to Christian theology which places a metaphor of pure love on the cross in the form of Jesus Christ and then reveals how he is tortured and killed, the Sacred Order of the Rosicrucians have placed a rose upon their version of the cross (the rose being a symbol of love and beauty) and teach how this flower may live and thrive.

Commonly known as "The Rose Cross" (Illus. 34), the symbol of the Rosicrucians is constructed of 6 squares that are meant to represent the unfolded form of a cube. The central square containing the rose would be the base of this cube, while the lowest square on the vertical column would represent the top after the four sides surrounding the rose were flipped up.

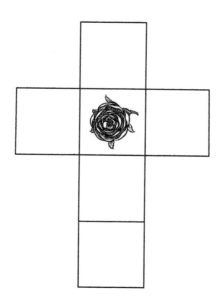

Illus. 34

As a Magickal symbol, the cube represents the four directions along with above and below, or the six perspectives of human perception. The cube is also a symbol of truth, yet truth expressed on the physical plane whereby it is also considered a symbol of the earth.

A cube is also used as a metaphor to represent the Sanctum Sanctorum or "Holy of Holies," the room in the Heavenly Temple that housed the Ark of the Covenant which contained the Shekinah or "Divine Presence." In the earthly Temple of King Solomon, the Sanctum Sanctorum contained only a "Stone of Foundation" a smaller cube that was supposed to represent individual human enlightenment in place of the Ark. The Qabalists knew this cube as the Stone of the Philosophers which they expressed with the word ABN or "Eben" whose translation is "a stone" and contains a coalescence of the words AB (Father) and BN (Son) or the Divine and Earthly consciousness. It is also said that the temple which houses this stone is not one made with hands. What is meant by the preceding statement is that every one of us is an embodiment of the earthly Temple of Solomon that houses the Stone of Foundation. With this in mind, the Rose Cross would then be a symbol that each human being is an expression of love (represented by the rose) with the Cross itself as the unfolded cube specifically referring to the universal consciousness within us through which this vibration will manifest.

❖❖❖

CHAPTER VII

SIGILS

NOTHER important tool in the creation of a Magickal Key involves a construction known as a "Sigil" which is an abstract symbol derived from a literal name that is supposed to represent the essence of a Deity, Angel, Demon, Spirit, or even a human being, in order to facilitate the connection between the Magician and whatever intelligence he or she may wish to summon.

Sigils are made by utilizing what are known as "Magic Squares" (or Qameas in Hebrew) of which there are seven corresponding to the heavenly bodies Saturn, Mars, Jupiter, Venus, Mercury, the Sun, and the Moon. Below is a diagram of the Magick Square of Saturn.

4	9	2
3	5	7
8	1	6

* The other 6 Magick Squares are listed in the Appendix.

What defines a Magick Square is that the added sum of any of its horizontal, vertical, or diagonal lines will reveal the same value, which in the case of the Square of Saturn is 15.

In order to create a Sigil from the Magick Square of Saturn, I would first need to determine the Being that I wanted to contact within the energy of Saturn and then I would need to trace a map of this Being's name within the Magick Square. In this case I will construct a Sigil for the Angel AGIAL who represents the Intelligence of Saturn. Before being able to draw this map, I must first reduce the name AGIAL to its numerical equivalent in Hebrew. Using Gematria, this would be done as follows;

A = Aleph = 1

G = Gimel = 3

I = Yod = 10

A = Aleph = 1

L = Lamed = 30

A glance back at the Square of Saturn will reveal that the highest number within that square is 9, which presents a problem because two of the letters in the name AGIAL have numerical values greater than 9 (specifically Yod equaling 10 and Lamed equaling 30). What needs to be done to remedy the situation is to utilize the Qabalah of the Nine Chambers to reduce the values of the pair of letters in question so that they will have values of 9 or less. In the table that illustrates the Nine Chambers, the box on the extreme right of the top row contains the letters Aleph (A), Yod (I), and Qoph (Q), while the box on the extreme left of the same row contains the letters Gimel (G), Lamed (L), and Shin

(Sh). What is necessary at this point is to replace the values of the letters Lamed and Yod with other values within their respective chambers so that the totals will be low enough to fit within the Magick Square of Saturn. Specifically the value of the letter Yod (10) will be replaced with the value of the letter Aleph (1) and the value of the letter Lamed (30) will be replaced with that of Gimel (3). At this point, the original numerical correspondences for AGIAL (1, 3, 10, 1, and 30) will be replaced with the new set of values (1, 3, 1, 1, and 3) adjusted through the use of the Qabalah of the Nine Chambers.

To trace the Sigil, one begins by drawing a small circle inside the numbered square corresponding to the first letter within the name. From there, a line is drawn, in order, to each subsequent number/letter until the name is completed. In the case of a letter being repeated, a small crook is made in the line before going on to the next letter. When the name has been completed, a small perpendicular dash is drawn to signify the end of the line. Below is the Sigil for AGIAL drawn in the Square of Saturn after having been transformed as per the Qabalah of the Nine Chambers.

The final step of the procedure would be to redraw the Sigil minus the Magick Square within the Talisman that is being created.

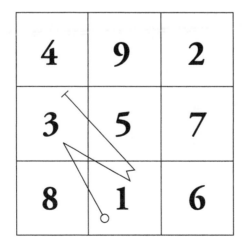

Illus. 35

Another method for constructing Sigils that should be mentioned briefly is the use of "The Rose of Twenty-Two Petals" a construction that is part of a larger diagram of "The Rose Cross" worn upon the lamen or silk collarette of the Adeptus Minor Grade within The Hermetic Order of the Golden Dawn. The Rose of Twenty-Two petals refers to the 22 letters of the Hebrew alphabet that are individually inscribed on each of the flower's petals. Illustration 36 is a reproduction of The Rose of 22 Petals.

THE ROSE OF TWENTY-TWO PETALS

Illus. 36

To create a Sigil using the Rose, one merely needs to trace a line from letter to letter within the flower, thereby eliminating the need to use different Magick Squares, or occasionally needing recourse to The Qabalah of the Nine Chambers to reduce the values of words that won't fit within a particular Square. The down side to using the Rose is that many believe the Planetary Squares have a stronger connection to the Sacred Knowledge of Antiquity, the Rose Cross of the Rosicrucians being a relatively modern interpretation of this Ancient Knowledge. Nevertheless, it is possible to create appropriate Sigils using either of the methods described and the individual Initiate should use the approach that he or she is most drawn to.

❖❖❖

PART III

ANCIENT MAGICKAL KEYS

CHAPTER VIII

TWO ANCIENT MANUSCRIPTS

OW that the three branches of Magickal language along with Sacred Shapes and Sigils have been discussed, let us next examine a pair of Ancient Hebrew manuscripts in order to see how the Magicians of the past used this information to construct Talismans for Ritual Work.

The first of the two manuscripts that I will talk about is entitled "The Key of Solomon the King" and contains a collection of Talismanic Seals known as "Pantacles" that are dedicated to the various planetary energies. This manuscript is also sometimes referred to as "The Greater Key of Solomon" owing to the fact that a companion grimoire exists known as The Lemegeton or "The Lesser Key of Solomon." This secondary manuscript was also known as "The Goetia" which is a Greek word referring to lower or Demonic Magick. As the reader might guess from the name, The Lemegeton was concerned with evoking the lower or Demonic energies and hence will not be discussed in this book. The exact author of The Greater Key of Solomon is unknown, although it is believed by some that the manuscript was written by the Great King Solomon himself who legend describes as being the greatest Magician of his time.

The second manuscript that will be discussed is known as "The Book of the Sacred Magick of Abramelin the Mage" and was transcribed by a Medieval Qabalist known only as Abraham of

Wurzburg who claimed to have acquired his knowledge from an Egyptian Magician named Abramelin. This book contains a collection of word grids known as "Acrostics" whose contents literally describe the powers they are designed to manifest.

Both of the above mentioned books were translated and edited by the late Samuel Liddell "MacGregor" Mathers (1854 - 1918) who along with Dr. William Wynn Westcott and Dr. Robert Woodman founded the legendary Hermetic Order of the Golden Dawn, a Rosicrucian style Magickal Society which included among its members some of the best creative minds in England at the beginning of the 20th Century. Credited with writing the majority of the rituals for the various grades within the Golden Dawn, Mathers was considered to be the most innovative Occult scholar of his time as well as a Master practitioner of the Magickal Arts.

The Talismans which appear in both of these Classic books are the stylistic forerunners of the Modern Keys I present in this volume; however, before I begin discussing the structure of these Ancient Keys, let me first make some brief points about the context in which this classical information should be considered. Although the reader will see the name of God mentioned quite frequently in the Talismans that will be analyzed from both of the respective manuscripts, it should be kept in mind that despite this rhetoric, the Ancient Adepts actually considered God to be more of a concept of Universal Unity and balance rather than a bearded Titan sitting on a throne in heaven. It is easy in these modern times to assume our sophistication over ancient peoples and then to facilitate this attitude by taking everything they wrote literally. Even though their style of literary composition may seem archaic and stiff by today's standards, the fact of the matter is that the Ancient Adepts were Masters of Metaphor, an Art modern people often disregard in favor of a scientific exactness whose precision ironically enough originates from conceptions that are usually quite metaphorical in their own rite.

The second point I want to make is that the Talismans we will be looking at from these two Ancient Manuscripts were used as elements in Ritual Workings, which means that there was a definite procedure executed around their utilization. This point is necessary to keep in mind because even though Talismans can be very powerful tools, ultimately they are nothing more than mere objects until they are infused with the essence of Spirit through the actions of the Magician.

THE KEY OF SOLOMON THE KING

Culled from a collection of manuscripts housed in the British Museum in London, "The Key of Solomon the King" was the result of extensive editing in which S.L. Mathers was not only required to translate multiple languages but also to do a certain amount of restoration on some of the glyphs within the Pantacle Keys that had deteriorated over time. Published in 1889, the book sold at that time for the price of 1.5 Pound Sterling, which nowadays would be roughly equal to approximately 300 dollars. Because of its high price and esoteric subject matter, the book did not sell well outside of Golden Dawn members, although it did manage to stay in print and in 1909 sales of a reissued edition benefited from some rather sensationalized publicity relating to a legal dispute between Mathers and Aleister Crowley (which Crowley won on appeal) regarding the publication of some of the secret Golden Dawn rituals in Crowley's magazine "The Equinox."

All told, "The Key of Solomon the King" consists of 44 Pantacles grouped under the headings of the seven heavenly bodies known at that time to the Ancient Adepts, namely Saturn, Jupiter, Mars, Venus, Mercury, The Sun, and The Moon. Other than "The First Pantacle of the Moon," all of the Keys are composed in a circular format, the lone exception being constructed in a rectangular shape that is meant to represent a doorway or a gate. The theory behind the Keys is that they were designed to give the user power over the lower spirits to perform certain tasks. This power was a result of the Keys having come directly from the masters of these Spirits, namely God and his Angels. Another aspect involved in the utilization of the Keys related to the purity and integrity of the user who was required not only to execute the proper rituals and prayers, but also to have engaged in the appropriate rights of consecration beforehand for both himself and the space that would house the operation. The directions for the construction of the Pantacles require that they be drawn by hand on virgin pieces of paper using the appropriate colors for the planets involved. It was also necessary for the Keys to only be constructed during the hours and days attributed to Mercury (the God of Magick) when the Moon was in an Air or Earth sign (i.e. Libra, Gemini, Aquarius, or Capricorn, Taurus, Virgo). Keep in mind that Mercury is the ruling planet for both Gemini and Virgo hence giving the Patron of Magick special powers in the elements of both Air (Gemini) and Earth (Virgo). Below is a pair of tables outlining the traditional Magickal and Planetary associations for each of the days of the week, so the reader will be able to see what days and hours the Ancients considered sacred to Mercury.

MAGICKAL ASSOCIATIONS FOR THE DAYS OF THE WEEK

Days	Monday	Tuesday	Wednesday	Thursday	Friday	Saturday	Sunday
Archangel	Gabriel	Khamael	Michael	Tzadiqel	Haniel	Tzaphqiel	Raphael
Angel	Gabriel	Zamel	Raphael	Sachiel	Anael	Cassiel	Michael
Planet	Moon	Mars	Mercury	Jupiter	Venus	Saturn	Sun
Metal	Silver	Iron	Mercury	Tin	Copper	Lead	Gold
Colour	White	Red	Purple or Mixed Colours	Blue	Green	Black	Yellow

Illus. 37

TABLE OF THE PLANETARY HOURS

Sunday	Monday	Tuesday	Wednesday	Hours from midnight to midnight	Thursday	Friday	Saturday
Merc.	Jup.	Ven.	Sat.	1	Sun.	Moon	Mars
Moon	Mars	Mer.	Jup.	2	Ven.	Sat.	Sun.
Sat.	Sun.	Moon	Mars	3	Mer.	Jup.	Ven.
Jup.	Ven.	Sat.	Sun.	4	Moon	Mars	Mer.
Mars	Mer.	Jup.	Ven.	5	Sat.	Sun.	Moon
Sun.	Moon	Mars	Mer.	6	Jup.	Ven.	Sat.
Ven.	Sat.	Sun	Moon	7	Mars	Mer.	Jup.
Mer.	Jup.	Ven.	Sat.	8	Sun	Moon	Mars
Moon	Mars	Merc.	Jup.	9	Ven.	Sat.	Sun
Sat.	Sun	Moon	Mars	10	Merc.	Jup.	Ven.
Jup.	Ven.	Sat.	Sun	11	Moon	Mars	Merc.
Mars	Merc.	Jup.	Ven.	12	Sat.	Sun	Moon
Sun	Moon	Mars	Merc.	1	Jup.	Ven.	Sat.
Ven.	Sat.	Sun	Moon	2	Mars	Merc.	Jup.
Merc.	Jup.	Ven.	Sat.	3	Sun	Moon	Mars
Moon	Mars	Merc.	Jup.	4	Ven.	Sat.	Sun
Sat.	Sun	Moon	Mars	5	Merc.	Jup.	Ven.
Jup.	Ven.	Sat.	Sun	6	Moon	Mars	Merc.
Mars	Merc.	Jup.	Ven.	7	Sat.	Sun	Moon
Sun	Moon	Mars	Merc.	8	Jup.	Ven.	Sat.
Ven.	Sat.	Sun.	Moon	9	Mars	Merc.	Jup.
Merc.	Jup.	Ven.	Sat.	10	Sun.	Moon	Mars
Moon	Mars	Mer.	Jup.	11	Ven.	Sat.	Sun
Sat.	Sun	Moon	Mars	12	Mer.	Jup.	Ven.

Illus. 38

What follows next is an analysis of a selection of Pantacle Keys from the Text of "The Key of Solomon the King."

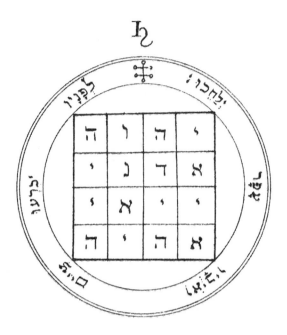

Illus. 39

Illustration 39 is the First Pantacle of Saturn and was utilized for striking terror into the spirits. Supposedly the operator had only to show this particular seal and any recalcitrant spirits would immediately kneel in obedience. The word grid in this Key is not an example of a perfect Acrostic (readable in any direction) but is instead normally legible as per the rules of Hebrew. The grid contains the 4 great names of God and reading from top to bottom and right to left these names are, IHVH (Tetragrammaton), ADNI (Adonai or "Lord"), IIAI (Yiai, which has the same Gematria as AL, another name of God), and AHIH (Eheieh or "Existence"). According to Mathers, the Hebrew verse written around the perimeter of the circle is from the Ninth Psalm and translates as "The Ethiopians shall kneel before him, His enemies shall lick the dust."

Illustration 40 is the Second Pantacle of Saturn and was supposedly of use in overcoming adversity. Unlike the word grid

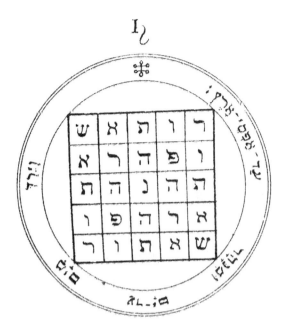

Illus. 40

in the previous Key that read only horizontally, this grid is an example of a perfect Acrostic and reads in all 4 directions. It is the Hebrew translation of the famous Magick Square, "SATOR AREPO TENET OPERA ROTAS" found in the ruins of the Roman city of Pompeii, and although many Historians and Occultists have tried their hands at translating the unusual words in this Square, I prefer the interpretation rendered by Mathers;

S	A	T	O	R	= The Creator
A	R	E	P	O	= slow-moving
T	E	N	E	T	= maintains
O	P	E	R	A	= His Creations
R	O	T	A	S	= as vortices

The grid in the Pantacle Key contains 25 squares so that if the number of Divine Unity (1) is added the total will then be 26, the numerical value of Tetragrammaton (IHVH). In addition, Mathers points out in his editorial comments that if the 25 letters comprising the verse around the perimeter are added together and then combined with the value of the word ALHIM (The One in the Many) their sum will be equal to that of the 25 Hebrew letters in the Magick Square. I was very excited upon first hearing this and immediately began a proof of Mathers assertion; however, after several tries over a period of two years, my calculations consistently revealed that the sum of the letters in the Magick squared totaled 3,258 while the values of the letters in the verse plus ALHIM came to 3,267. I am not pointing this mistake out in an attempt to criticize Mathers but rather to alert other scholars that perhaps in the subsequent printings of this Master Work from its first edition one of the letters had been inadvertently eliminated or changed from the original text. Since the discrepancy between the totals of the two words is 9, the value of the Hebrew letter Teth or "T" which translates as "A Serpent", then maybe the uncovering of this discrepancy will lead to some other bit of knowledge previously hidden in the original manuscript, as the Serpent is the animal totem associated with the sign of Scorpio which is the energy that rules investigations as well esoteric Occult knowledge.

Illustration 41 is the Second Pantacle of Mars, which was to be used for dealing successfully with all types of diseases when it is applied to the imbalanced area. In the center of the circle is a 6-pointed Star or "Hexagram" the Sacred Geometric figure symbolizing "As Above, So Below" while in each of the points of the star is a rendering of the Hebrew letter "Heh" which translates as "A Window." In the central hexagon of the star are three Hebrew words. Across the top is IHVH (Tetragrammaton) and across the bottom is ALHIM (The many in the One). Linking these two words is a vertical rendering of the word YHShVH or "Yeheshuah" (Jesus).

According to Mathers, the verse around the perimeter of the

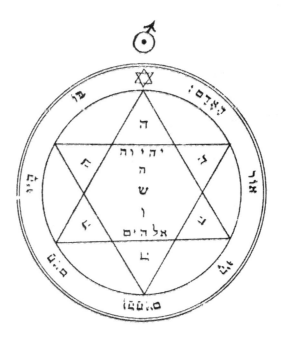

Illus. 41

circle reads "In Him was life, and the life was the light of man." Thus in this Talisman, one can see the attempt to create a window to connect the earthly reality of humanity with the Higher Balance inherent in the power of Divine Creation.

The last Pantacle from "The Key of Solomon the King" that I will discuss is the Third Pantacle of Jupiter (Illus. 42), which was used to defend those who invoked the Spirits. It was believed that at the sight of this seal, a Spirit would become obedient and listen. The inner area of this seal is divided into 4 sections. In the upper left quadrant is the Magickal Seal of the Planet Jupiter, which has the letters IHVH inscribed within its circular emblem, and in the quadrant on the lower left is the Sigil for the Intelligence of Jupiter (the Angel Iophiel). In the quadrant on the upper right is the name, ADNI or "Adonai," which translates as "Lord" and in the lower right section is the Tetragrammaton (IHVH). Mathers translates the verse around the perimeter as "They that trust in God shall be as Mount Zion, which cannot be removed, but will last forever."

Illus. 42

❖❖❖

THE BOOK OF THE SACRED MAGICK OF ABRAMELIN THE MAGE

Translated from a manuscript discovered by S.L. Mathers in the Bibliotheque de L'Arsenal in Paris, "The Book of the Sacred Magick of Abramelin the Mage" is considered to be the most legendary piece of Magickal writing to come out of the Great Esoteric Revival at the beginning of the 20th Century. This reputation is a result of both the sense of mystery that surrounds the book's original author along with the unusual happenings that befell Mathers while he was working on the translation. Several of his Magickal contemporaries were in awe of the manuscript, among them Aleister Crowley and William Butler Yeats, both of who believed that Mathers was taking a great risk by attempting to reveal this information to the general public. For both Crowley and Yeats this risk was of a Spiritual nature, and the incidents that subsequently transpired during the time Mathers was working on the book would appear to support his colleague's suspicions. From the beginning, Mathers had nothing but trouble with the project. After completing the first draft of his translation the manuscript was mysteriously misplaced so that he was forced to begin again from scratch, and then while redoing the work he experienced several unexplainable bicycle accidents on the Paris roads so that eventually he was forced to give up riding and was reduced to walking. Finally published in 1898, the Abramelin Book is now considered a masterpiece by those knowledgeable in the Occult, yet at the time of its initial release it sold poorly and brought Mathers very little recognition for his efforts.

"The Book of the Sacred Magick of Abramelin the Mage" was originally written by a Medieval Qabalist known only as Abraham of Wurzburg who claims that the information he is recounting was obtained during his travels in Egypt from an Egyptian Mage by the name of Abramelin. Written as a Hermetic legacy to his youngest Son and thus not intended for a general audience, Abraham's manuscript is divided into three sections consisting of an Introduction, Preparatory Instructions for the Magician, and a large collection of Acrostic Talismans.

The Introduction begins with Abraham's youth and then continues with his subsequent travels as a young man throughout Europe and North Africa in search of Magickal Knowledge. After encountering Abramelin and learning the Egyptian's secrets, the remainder of the Introduction is concerned with a recount of the Historical events Abraham claims to have affected by using the esoteric knowledge bequeathed to him. Regarding this aspect of the narrative, Mathers comments in his editorial preface "He (Abraham) stands a dim and shadowy figure behind the tremendous complication of central European upheaval at that terrible and instructive epoch; as Adepts of his type always appear and always have appeared upon the theatre of history in great crises of nations." From the dates offered in the Introduction, it can be concluded that Abraham was a contemporary of the famous Alchemist Nicholas Flamel and the legendary Christian Rosenkruetz, while the historical figures he claims to have worked both for and against were, The Emperor Sigismund of Germany, The Duke of Bavaria, Pope John XXIII, and Pope Gregory XII.

The second section of the book is concerned with personal rites of purification for the Magician so that the individual may gain conversation with one's Holy Guardian Angel. The reason for this conversation is so that afterwards one may utilize the power and authority of the Angel to command the lower or "Demonic" Spirits to do one's bidding. According to Abraham, the way of initially approaching such a mystical conversation was to cleanse one's body and spirit through a systematic process that involved a retirement from the material world for a period of 6 months. After this retreat of cleansing, devotions, and prayers, if one were still sincere (and who wouldn't be after 6 months) then the person's Holy Guardian Angel would appear and grant power over the Demons. The Talismans contained in the final section of the book would then come into play as instructions for the Demons to follow.

Of course in Psychological terms, the concept of a Holy Guardian Angel would represent the Higher or more evolved aspects of the individual, while the Demons would correspond to the lower portions of human nature with the essence of the whole process being to gain mastery over the self from the highest possible vantage point. This concept of gaining mastery over the self was something I used to explain the practice of Magick back in Chapter I when I intimated that one could not hope to invoke the power of The Goddess Venus if love did not exist first within the person performing the operation. The second section of the Abramelin book also goes a long way in dispelling many of the misguided notions of what Magick is and isn't in that it centers the source of power within the individual and portrays the manifestations of the material world as being an extension of what exists within the person.

Unlike the Pantacles in "The Key of Solomon the King," none of the talismans in the third and final section of the Abramelin book utilize diagrams, sacred shapes, or the circular Pantacle format. All of the talismans of Abramelin are square word grids known as "Acrostics" of which there are 4 major types. The first type consists of the entire square being filled with letters so that it resembles a completed crossword puzzle. The second type consists of only part of the square being filled with letters. The third type involves the letters forming a border around the edge of the square and the fourth type is when the letters are randomly placed within the square.

Illustration 43 is an example of a Perfect Acrostic (readable in all four directions), and one of the first of the four types mentioned, which is in turn part of a larger group of talismans for knowing all manner of things past and future as long as the knowledge sought is not opposed to God or his most Holy Will.

According to S.L Mathers, the word NABHI contained in the first horizontal line of the grid is derived from the root NBA, meaning "To prophesize." The word on the second horizontal line is ADAIH, derived from the Hebrew root DIH or "a bird of

omen." The third word is BAKAB and means "trouble" while the fourth word is HIADA from the root IDH meaning "to be sent forward or thrown." The last word is IHBAN and is from the root IHB meaning "to bring." An approximate narrative translation of the aforementioned words could therefore be "To bring omens that will prophesize future trouble."

To activate this talisman the text states that one should place it under their hat or on the top of their head after which the spirit involved will carry out the activity specified in the acrostic.

Also of the first type, Illustration 44 is additionally a perfect acrostic and bears a notable resemblance to the renowned SATOR AREPO TENET OPERA ROTAS which was discussed previously in the analysis of the Second Pantacle of Saturn from

Illus. 44

"The Key of Solomon the King." While King Solomon's version was designed to repress the pride of the Spirits, this talisman was supposedly useful in arousing the affection of a maiden. Below is the translation offered by Mathers for each of the words in this grid as it appears within the Abramelin book.

S A L O M = Peace
A R E P O = he distills
L E M E L = unto fullness
O P E R A = upon the dry ground
M O L A S = quick motion

A liberal summation of the foregoing translation might be "He quickly distills peace and fullness in a previously unfertile place" no doubt referring to sowing the seeds of one's affections with the intended maiden.

To activate this talisman it is necessary to say aloud the name of the person you wish to affect and, if possible, to even go as far as to touch them with a written copy of it.

G	I	L	I	O	N	I	N
I							
L							
I							
O							
N							
I							
N							

Illus. 45

Illustration 45 is of the second type and is included within a group intended "For Diverse Visions." Specifically this grid is for obtaining images in crystals, glasses, or mirrors, and the word GILIONIN is appropriately the Chaldean word for "a mirror." No special instructions are given for the activation of this talisman.

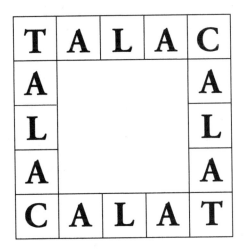

Illus. 46

The word TALAC translates from Hebrew as "thy mists." This talisman (Illus. 46) is an example of the third of the four types mentioned earlier and is part of a group that was to be used for making one invisible. There are a dozen keys in this group with one each corresponding to the twelve hours of both the day and night. This particular example is marked as number 11, which I assume means it should be used if one wants to be invisible at either 11 a.m. or 11 p.m.

According to Abraham it is very simple to activate this talisman, simply put it on top of your head when you wish to be invisible and then remove it when you wish to be seen.

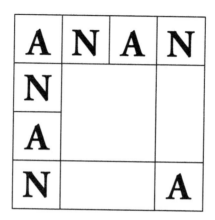

Illus. 47

Illustration 47 is an example of the fourth type of acrostic and is in turn part of a larger group designed to afford the Magician the ability to fly. The word ANAN means "great labor" and the singular letter in the corner is the Hebrew letter Aleph, the first letter of the Hebrew alphabet that is often used by Qabalists as a symbol for the element of Air. Thus this talisman will provide a great effort to propel the Magician through the air.

To activate this talisman, one must first say aloud the place you intend to go. Next the symbol must then be put on one's head being especially careful at all times to make sure that it doesn't fall off for the results of such a mistake could be very dangerous. It is further recommended (I believe somewhat tongue in cheek) not to use this symbol at night or in bad weather.

❖❖❖

PART IV

MODERN MAGICKAL KEYS

CHAPTER IX

ACROSTICS

N this chapter I will present a series of original acrostics made of Hebrew letters grouped into various Sacred Shapes. All of these shaped word constructions are a result of channeled information and came about as a direct product of Magickal Ritual Work. The analysis that accompanies each of these talismans utilizes the various Magickal Languages covered earlier in this book, the purpose being to serve as an instructional guide for those who may feel inspired to attempt to create their own acrostic talismans.

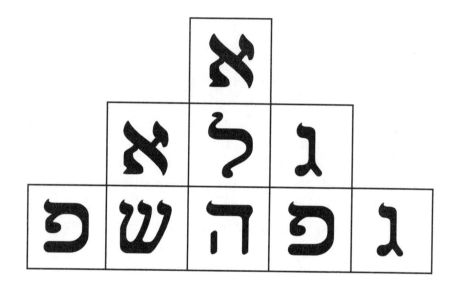

Illus. 48

THE KEY OF THE GREAT WORK

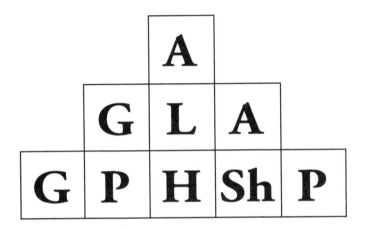

Illus. 49

What is the purpose of life? I believe that as human beings, the reason we are alive is to learn and grow. But to learn what, and to grow towards where? In his writings, Aleister Crowley often referred to "The Great Work" which is the Spiritual process that an individual must undergo in order to realize his or her true place in the overall scheme of the universe. Right now you may be wondering about your true purpose in this life. For many years this was a question that caused me a great deal of consternation although now my daily activities as a Psychic Counselor and Teacher along with projects such as this book have provided me with the answer. I have found that the pursuit of The Great Work is the path to self-discovery and self-realization, which essentially means taking responsibility for being the creator of your life and all the things in it. What follows is a talisman that can be used as a meditative guide for understanding the process of self-realization as it is defined within the Western Esoteric System or "Magick."

Rather than approaching a translation of "The Key of the Great Work" from the standpoint of going through it as though it were being read line by line, I have instead grouped the letters of this Key into a central cross with a triad situated on each side.

The first of these sections I will translate is the central cross, which in turn consists of two parts: the middle vertical column that extends from the apex to the base of the overall triangle, and the second line of the Key that would form the horizontal arms of the proposed cross. The middle vertical column contains the word ALH which means "Goddess." From a Qabalistic perspective, this word is particularly intriguing for it is actually three words in one. The initial letter A (Aleph) is the first letter of the Hebrew alphabet and is often used to symbolize the consciousness of the One Infinite Creator. If the second letter L is then added to A, the resulting word will be AL a Hebrew name for God the Father. Thus within the word ALH or "Goddess" there exists the Supernal Triad of Female, Male, and Unity as depicted in the Tree of Life.

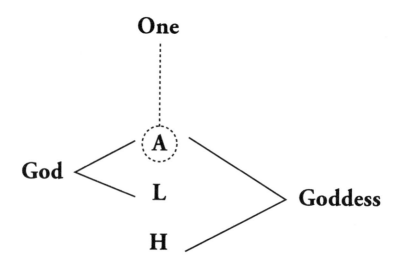

Illus. 50

Additionally, the letter at the base of the column H (Heh) translates as "a window" which would then represent the window of enlightenment that offers a view of Supreme Unity.

The Central Cross is then completed by adding the word GLA contained in the second horizontal line, which translate as "to reveal."

Illus. 51

The other sections of the Key that remain to be translated are the triads on either sides of the cross, which are demarcated by the dotted lines in the following diagram.

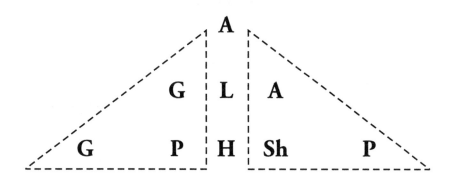

Illus. 52

The triangle on the left consists of the letters G P G which form both a horizontal and vertical spelling of the word GP or "Self." The triangle on the right contains a pair of inter-locking words ASh or "Fire" and AShP or "Magician."

I will now take these three separate shapes that have been isolated within the overall acrostic (the cross & the 2 triangles) and use them to present an interpretation for the meaning of this Key.

Beginning with the two triangles:

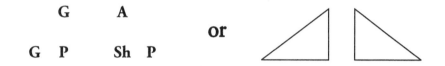

G   A
G P   Sh P   **or**

Illus. 53

"The duality of existence (GP twice, or a dual "self") illuminated by the cleansing fire (ASh) of Magick (the Magician, AShP)."

Next the Central Cross:

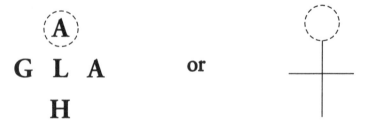

A
G L A   **or**
H

Illus. 54

"The window of enlightenment (H) revealing (GLA) the Holy Supernal Triad (ALH) leading to the One (A)."

The combined meanings of the triangles and the cross can then subsequently be viewed as a summation of the intentions behind the pursuit of The Great Work by a practicing Ritual Magician.

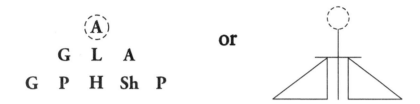

"The duality of existence (GPG) illuminated by the cleansing fire (ASh) of Magick (the Magician, AShP) whereby the window (H) of enlightenment reveals (GLA) The Holy Supernal Triad (ALH) leading to the One (A)."

The following Gematria correspondences for "The Key of the Great Work" have been computed based on the three sections that were established in the translation rather than just taking an overall tally of the letters involved.

In the first triangle, I went beyond the straight values of the three letters involved (G P G) and instead computed the total to reflect the two words spelled within the triad (GP and GP).

GP + GP = (3 + 80) + (3 + 80) = 166 = OLIVN or "the most high".

The number 166 can also be reduced to 1 + 6 + 6 or 13, the numerical value of the word AHBH or "Love."

In the second triangle the values have again been computed to reflect the fact that there are multiple words formed by the initial three letters (A, Sh, P).

ASh + AShP = (1 + 300) + (1 + 300 + 80) = 682 or 6 + 8 + 2 = 16 = AZVB or "Hyssop" a plant used in Hebrew purification rituals.

In the central cross I again computed values for all the interlocking words rather than just logging the values of the basic 6 letters:

A			**A**	(1)	= 1
G L A	**or**		**AL**	(1 + 30)	= 31
H			**ALH**	(1 + 30 + 5)	= 36
			GLA	(3 + 30 + 1)	= <u>34</u>
					102

Total 102 = the value of 2 different Hebrew words,

AMVNH or "Faith" and TzBI or "Grace"

The message to be derived from a synthesis of all the preceding Gematria information can then be summarized in the following diagram and caption:

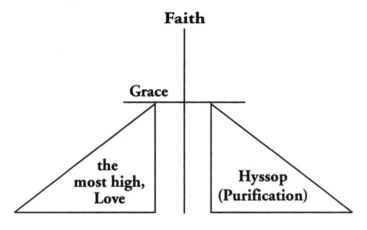

Illus. 56

"Love is the purifying Grace leading to True Faith "

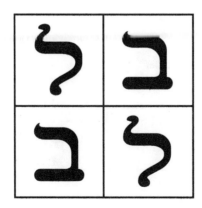

Illus. 57

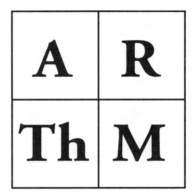

A	R
Th	M

A	D
Th	N

B	L
L	B

Illus. 58

THE KEY OF THE 13TH PATHWAY

This Key takes its name from the 13th Pathway on the Tree of Life that connects the spheres of Tiphareth and Kether. The Qabalistic title for this path is "The Uniting Intelligence" and it is associated with the journey of the Mystic toward Higher Consciousness. Three 4-letter acrostic squares constitute this Key, each of which is meant to correspond to the three major landmarks along the 13th Pathway. The top acrostic formed by the letters A, R, Th, and M represents the sphere of Kether or "The Crown" on the Tree of Life and the lowest of the three word squares formed by the letters B L B and L is intended to represent the sphere of Tiphareth or "The Heart Sphere." The middle square of A, D, Th, and N is intended to correspond to the Sphere which is not properly a Sephirah, namely Daath or "Knowledge." Situated over the throat, Daath is also referred to by Qabalists as "The Abyss" for knowledge can indeed be an abyss for those addicted to the trappings of the mind, hence it is in this mysterious sphere where our deepest life lessons are lying in wait because in order to truly know something it is often necessary to first embrace that which is unknown. The resulting journey along the 13th Pathway then becomes the unification of the heart energy of Tiphareth with that of the Higher Self residing in Kether by way of passing through the symbolic "Dark Night of the Soul" residing within the realm of Daath.

The first of the three acrostics I will discuss is the one corresponding to the sphere of Tiphareth. Composed of the letters B L, and L B, the translation of this square can be broken down as follows: BL means "Lord" and LB means "Heart." This would be considered a perfect acrostic in that it reads both horizontally and vertically, forwards and backwards. In addition "The Lord of the Heart" serves as a perfect literal description for the sphere of Tiphareth.

The second acrostic that corresponds to Daath or "The Abyss" is comprised of the letters A, D, Th, and N and the translations of the various words formed by these letters are:

Horizontal	AD	=	"mist"
	ThN	=	"The Great Dragon"
Vertical	ATh	=	"essence"
	DN	=	"to wander"
Diagonal	AN	=	"Where to?"
	DTh	=	"Faith"

A cohesive narrative statement that could then be constructed utilizing these different meanings would be "The dictates of true Faith require us all to wander through the mist and confront The Great Dragon of The Abyss. To Where? In search of our highest essence." Certainly an appropriate description of what Daath is supposed to represent in its position on the 13th Pathway.

The uppermost acrostic corresponding to the sphere of Kether and consisting of the letters A, R, Th, and M can be translated as follows:

Horizontal	AR	=	"light"
	ThM	=	"perfect"
Vertical	ATh	=	"essence"
	RM	=	"high, lofty"

From the preceding meanings, a fine description of the sphere of Kether can be had which would read "The perfect light of the higher essence."

At this point, let's construct a table for the combined translations of "The Key of the 13th Pathway."

A R

Th M   (Kether) The Perfect light
         of the Higher Self

A D

Th N   (Daath) True faith is that we all
         must wander through the mist
         and confront the Great Dragon
         of The Abyss in search of our
         Highest Essence.

B L

L B   (Tiphareth) The Lord of the Heart

A statement summarizing "The Key of the 13th Pathway" from the above information could then be: "The Lord of the Heart confronts the Great Dragon of the Abyss to attain the essence of the perfect light of the Higher Self."

The format I employed to compute the Gematria for this Key was to tally the values both horizontally and vertically for each square. As a result, instead of being limited to the words AR and ThM in the top square representing Kether I could now include the values of the words ATh and RM as well.

Horizontal values   A R or (1+ 200)   = 201

                   Th M or (400 + 40)   = 440

Vertical values   A Th or (1 + 400)   = 401

                   R M or (200 + 40)   = <u>240</u>

                      Total   1282

Because there were no sufficient correspondences to the value of 1,282, I instead chose to reduce the figure to 1 + 2 + 8 + 2 or 13. A Hebrew word with a value of 13 that is relevant to the meaning associated with the sphere of Kether is AChD or "Unity."

Using the same formula, the second acrostic that is meant to represent the sphere of Daath can be calculated as follows;

Horizontal values	A D	or (1 + 4)	=	5
	Th N	or (400 + 50)	=	450
Vertical values	A Th	or (1 + 400)	=	401
	D N	or (4 + 50)	=	<u>54</u>
		Total		910

The amount of 910 corresponds to the Hebrew word, RshIT or "Beginning." If 910 is then reduced to 9 + 1+ 0 or 10, its new value would correspond to the number associated with the earth sphere of Malkuth or "Kingdom" on the Tree of Life which is significant of both grounding and completion. In combining these translations of both the normal and manipulated meanings associated with 910, the results are "beginning" and "completion" relating to the full, transformative journey of the 13th Pathway through Daath.

The final square in "The Key of the 13th Pathway" corresponds to the sphere of Tiphareth on the Tree of Life and consists of the words BL and LB. Since there are only two letters in this square, the values of the vertical words will be exactly the same as those of the horizontal words. With this in mind, if I were to follow the same format as with the previous two squares, I would only need to double the value of either the horizontal or vertical words to arrive at my total:

Horizontal values   B L   or (2 + 30)   =   32

L B   or (30 + 2)   =   <u>32</u>

Total   64

(Vertical values)   <u>x2</u>

128

The number 128 has the same Gematria as the phrase YHVH AMVNH or "Faith in God." If we then reduce 128 to 1 + 2 + 8 or 11, we then have the numerical value of the Hebrew words AVD or "The Divine Light" and DHB or "Gold." Thus in the heart sphere of Tiphareth is "The Golden Light of Faith in God."

The total amount of all 3 squares combined equals 2,320 (1,282 + 910 + 128). This number can then be reduced to 232 (IHI AVR or "Let there be Light") and 0, which would then be symbolic of the Great Void and infinite darkness of The Abyss. With the aforementioned light we can then traverse the Abyss and reduce 232 to 2 + 3+ 2 or 7, by which we now gain equality with AHA, a notariqon (acronym) for Adonai Ha-Aretz or "The Lord of the Earth."

As a Healing tool, this Key can be of value in dealing with the stress surrounding our life lessons for it encodes into the auric field of whoever uses it, a higher understanding of the Hero's (or Heroine's) Journey and the obstacles inherent in such a path. This Key can also be used by Healers to recharge their batteries as it both strengthens and reaffirms the connection between the heart and the Crown through which Healing Power is channeled from Higher Sources.

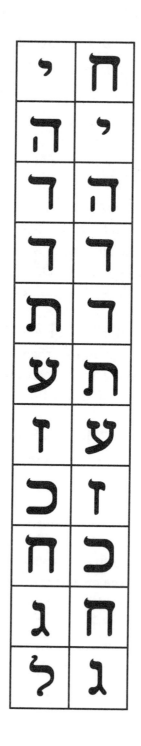

Illus. 59

THE KEY OF THE SERPENT

Ch	I
I	H
H	D
D	D
D	Th
Th	O
O	Z
Z	K
K	Ch
Ch	G
G	L

Illus. 60

There are two reasons for the name of this Key: the first is because the arrangement of the letters on the page resembles the form of a snake, and the second is because all of the two letter words included in the design read both horizontally and vertically so that their literal progression intimates the undulating movement of a serpent. To illustrate how this serpentine dynamic works within the Key, I will begin by translating the words at the bottom of the column and then move upwards.

At the base (or tail) of the serpent the first horizontal word is GL which translates as "a Spring or Fountain." The next horizontal word is ChG or "a circulatory form." This same pair of words are then spelled vertically as well, thus literally creating the beginning of a circulatory action like that of a spring or fountain which would initiate the beginning of the double helix created by the intertwining serpents in a caduceus.

Moving up the column, the next horizontal word is KCh which translates as "Power." Here we see the circulatory form expressed in the first two words perpetuated as the succeeding pair formed between KCh and the previous word ChG continue the original circular motion giving it power as one reads upward.

With the inclusion of a fourth word, a second quadrant of letters is created which has its own interior dynamic just as the first quadrant did; however, this second group is also linked with the previous quadrant like bricks being stacked to create a wall. The second quadrant consists of the previously mentioned KCh or "power" along with the word ZK or "purity." With the addition of these two words, the reader can now see that the original circulatory form is gaining both "power" and "purity" as it rises higher.

At this point, to avoid the possibility of losing the reader (and myself) in a maze of description, I will instead continue this explanation of "The Key of the Serpent" in the form of a diagram (Illus. 61):

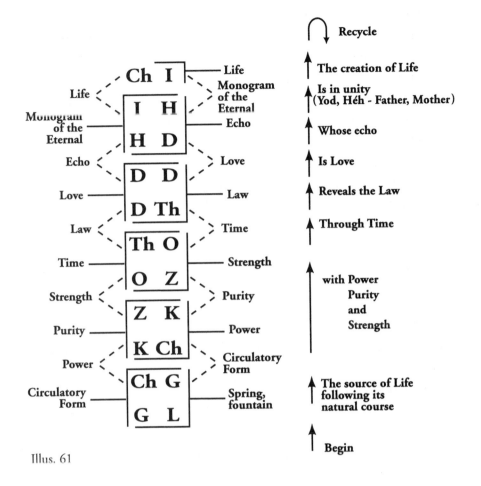

Illus. 61

It is also interesting to note that If lines are drawn to demarcate the various words along the column (keeping in mind that each of these words are both interlocked and repeated within those that precede and those that follow) what results is a graphic representation that looks very much like a spinal chord and its vertebrae (Illus. 62). This is poignant because in Tantric and Hindu Mysticism, the Kundalini or "Serpent " Energy that represents the life force of the individual resides at the base of the spine. Upon activation through either sexual union or meditation, this energy then travels upward along the spine to the Crown center at the top of the head where it explodes into enlightenment:

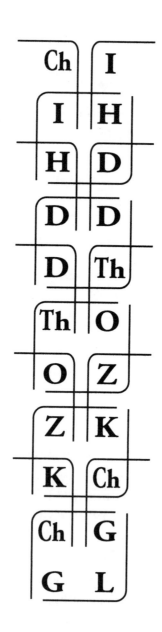

Illus. 62

To compute the Gematria correspondences for "The Key of the Serpent" I simply took the 11 words in the Key and assigned them their normal numerical values in Hebrew:

Ch	I	or	8 + 10	=	18
I	H	or	10 + 5	=	15
H	D	or	5 + 4	=	9
D	D	or	4 + 4	=	8
D	Th	or	4 + 400	=	404
Th	O	or	400 + 70	=	470
O	Z	or	70 + 7	=	77
Z	K	or	7 + 20	=	27
K	Ch	or	20 + 8	=	28
Ch	G	or	8 + 3	=	11
G	L	or	3 + 30	=	<u>33</u>

		Total	1100

Being a rather large total, I began by breaking down the figure of 1100 into 11 X 100. Equaling the value of 11 is the word AVD which represents the Divine light of the One Infinite Creator as it is expressed through the practice of Magick, and equaling the value of 100 is the literal spelling of the Hebrew letter Kaph or "KP."

Assigned to the 21st Pathway on the Tree of Life that connects the spheres of Chesed and Netzach, the letter Kaph is also attributed "The Wheel of Fortune" from the Tarot, a card whose meaning is associated with the natural cycles of death and rebirth. When it is fully spelled out, Kaph (KP) also represents a sublime example of Notariqon in Greek Qabalah with the initial "K" standing for the Greek word "Kteis" or the female genitalia, and the final "P" signifying the first letter in the Greek word "Phallos" or phallus. As a result of this information, Practical Qabalists consider the word Kaph to be a Magical formula for the unifying of duality on the earthly plain. If we now create an equation adding in the literal interpretations for 1100 = 11 X 100 the result would be:

$$1100 \quad = \quad 11 \quad X \quad 100$$

1100	=	11		100
The Key of the Serpent		AVD The Divine Light (Kundalini Energy)	of	KP Sacred Sexuality

Some suitable uses for this Key would include (1) using it as a focus for meditation to activate one's Kundalini (2) using it as a Feng-Shui tool to enhance the energy within a space where people are engaging in loving intimacy with Sacred Healing intentions (3) incorporating it as a Healing Tool (like a crystal or a gem stone) to aid individuals who are not maintaining an effective spiral-like flow of their Chi force.

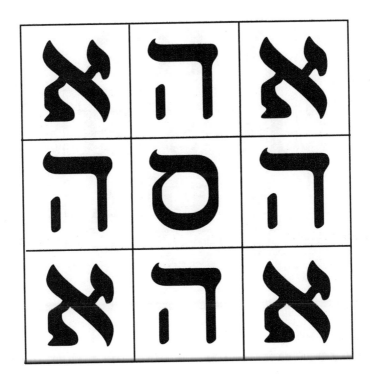

Illus. 63

THE KEY OF PRAYER

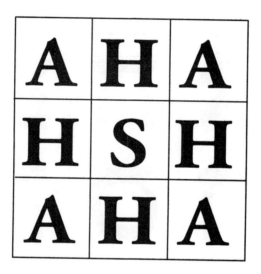

Illus. 64

Of the keys covered so far, this is the first classically perfect acrostic because of the additional feature that The Key of Prayer can also be read diagonally. The top horizontal line consists of the word AHA, which has been mentioned previously and is a Notariqon (acronym) derived from the phrase, Adonai Ha-Aretz or "The Lord of the Earth." The second horizontal line contains the word HSH or "Be silent" while the third horizontal line is a repeat of the first. Each of the vertical lines mirror their horizontal counterparts and subsequently translate exactly the same. Both diagonal lines consist of the word ASA which translates into English as "Healing" and reads both forwards and backwards.

Now that "The Key of Prayer" has been translated, let's next identify a few basic forms within its structure to uncover some additional levels of meaning.

I will begin by considering the letters that form the outer perimeter of the square:

A	H	A		The Omnipresence
H		H	or	of God
A	H	A		(Lord of the Earth)

The central letter of the acrostic that is missing is Samekh (S), which is associated with the 25th Pathway on The Tree of Life and is attributed the Tarot Card of Temperance XIV, the Angel of the deck, which is symbolic of attaining perfection and balance through a reconciliation of opposites. The Egyptian correspondence to this Pathway is that of "Asar-Un-Nefer" or the concept of humanity perfected in the image of God. With this in mind, the symbolism of "S" within the grid represents the aspirations of each human being to connect with the concept of a Higher Self as expressed by the Divine prototype of AHA.

The next step will be to look at the letters that form a cross within the overall square:

$$\begin{matrix} & H & \\ H & S & H \\ & H & \end{matrix}$$

HSH means "Be silent" hence this is a cross of silence whose center is Higher aspiration represented by "S".

The third step of this analysis involves looking at the "X" formed by the repeated diagonal spelling of "ASA."

```
       A       A
           S
       A       A
```

By indulging one's imagination just a bit, the above diagram can be perceived as an overhead view of a pyramid making this figure a construct of "Healing" topped with a capstone of "S" representing balance.

A summation of the preceding analysis could therefore be "The Higher Self within each of us can be aspired to through the silent meditation of prayer with the result being the attainment of healing through balance."

Now let us consider the Gematria for "The Key of Prayer."

Horizontal values: AHA (1 + 5 + 1) = 7
HSH (5 + 60 + 5) = 70
AHA (1 + 5 + 1) = 7

Total   84

Some Hebrew words with the numerical total of 84 are ChLVM or "a dream" and IDO or "Knew." The number 84 can also be reduced to 7 X 12 or the number of the Goddess Venus (7), multiplied by the 12 Houses or signs of the Zodiac, thus the manifestation of the Pure Love of the Universe.

The vertical values in The Key of Prayer are the same as the horizontal values (84) and if we add them both together the resulting sum is 168. This number can then in turn be broken down into 100 + 68 in order to yield the following correspondences:

100 = MDVN or "an effort or an exertion"

68 = ChKM or "to be wise"

The diagonal values are a repeat of the word ASA (1 + 60 + 1) and doubling this total would give us the number 124. A Hebrew word with the value of 124 is ORN or "Eden".

The total of the combined horizontal and vertical values (168) plus the combined diagonal values (124) yields a sum of 292 which is in turn the value of both BTzR or "harvest" and RPVAH or "Medicine."

From all of the preceding Gematria information, a narrative description of "The Key of Prayer" might be "Prayer is the conscious effort (MDVN) to connect with our Higher Knowing (ChKM and IDO) so as to realize the Love of the Universe (7 X 12) and its perfection (ORN) to attain the enlightened dream (ChLVM) of a Higher Healing (BTzR and RPVAH).

Some practical applications for this Key could include (1) making it a focal point during meditation or merely exhibiting it somewhere in the space where one meditates (2) in Healing Circles copies of The Key of Prayer could be offered as a handout among the participants (3) keeping the Key on one's person could serve as a reminder to be focused on the Higher good during the course of the day.

There are undoubtedly many possible uses for "The Key of Prayer" though probably the aspect I enjoy most about this Key is that it presents a coherent, referenced explanation of the dynamics of prayer and why it should work!

Illus. 65

THE KEY OF QABALISTIC CROSS

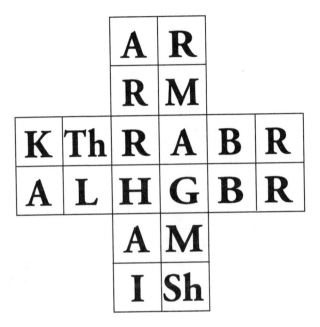

Illus. 66

To avoid unnecessary confusion and to better facilitate translation and analysis, I have decided to divide "The Key of the Qabalistic Cross" into a diagram of 3 separate sections:

```
        A  R
               >  Section 1
        R  M

K Th  R  A  B  R
                      >  Section 2
A  L  H  G  B  R

        A  M
               >  Section 3
        I  Sh
```

Illus. 67

The first section consists of the top 4 letters of the Cross A R R M which interlock to form a pair of words that read both horizontally and vertically. Following is a diagram that illustrates how the letters of this first section are grouped along with their English translations:

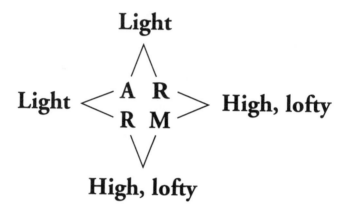

The second section is made up of the 12 letters within the two lines that form the horizontal arms of the Cross. The six letters comprising the first line are K, Th, R, A, B, and R and within this line two words can be constructed. The first is KThR or "Kether" the name of the first sphere on The Tree of Life which translates as "Crown" and the second word is ABR which is a Notariqon (acronym) for Ab, Ben, Ruach or "Father, Son, and Holy Spirit." The second line of this section contains the letters A, L, H, G, B, and R which can be grouped to spell a pair of words. The first is ALH or "Goddess" and the second is GBR or "A Mighty Hero."

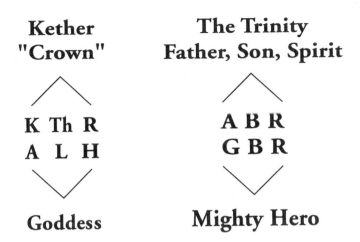

Kether
"Crown"

K Th R
A L H

Goddess

The Trinity
Father, Son, Spirit

A B R
G B R

Mighty Hero

Illus. 69

The final section of the Cross to be translated is the base which consists of the letters, A, M, I, and Sh. There are 4 words formed by these letters and they are AM or "Mother", ShM or "The Name", Ish or "Essence", and AI or "Island." Below is a diagram showing how the letters are grouped together and the subsequent words they form:

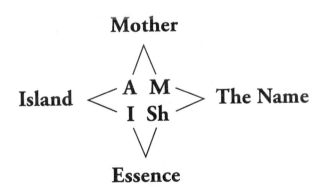

Mother

Island ← A M → The Name
         I Sh

Essence

Illus. 70

At this point, I think it would be prudent to pause for a moment to consider an overall view of the Cross and the translations of the various words it contains:

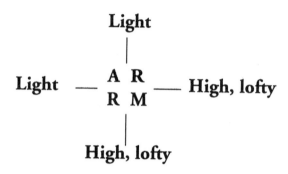

Kether (Crown) - K Th R   A B R - Holy Trinity
                                                    (Father, Son Spirit)

        Goddess - A L H   G B R - Mighty Hero

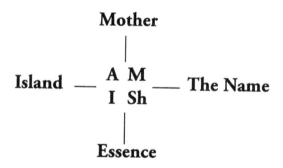

Now that "The Key of the Qabalistic Cross" has been translated, my intention is to show how the 10 spheres of The Tree of Life are contained esoterically within the words that form the Cross.

THE TREE OF LIFE

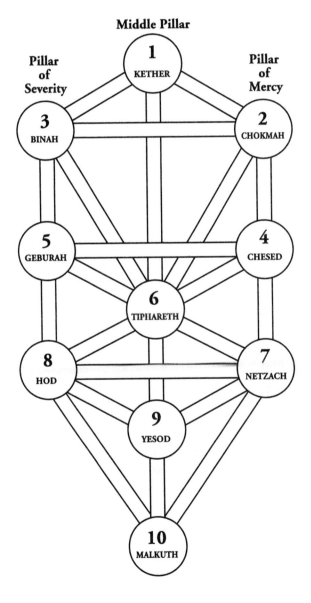

Illus. 72

Before I begin to draw any connections between The Key of the Qabalistic Cross and The Tree of Life, it will first be necessary to briefly introduce a concept from the Qabalah known as "The Great Egg." To illustrate this concept I have constructed the following diagram of 3 concentric circles:

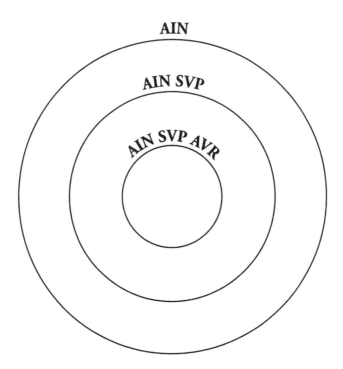

Illus. 73

The reader will undoubtedly notice that a Hebrew name has been assigned to each of the three circles in the preceding diagram. The name of the outermost circle is AIN meaning "The negative or non-existent" and is meant to correspond to the Great Void or The Great Darkness where all potential exists before anything is realized. The name of the central circle is AIN SVP or "Ain Soph" and translates as "The Limitless." This circle corresponds to the point within the Great Void that has become aware of its own existence and would correlate to what many refer to as "God." The name of the innermost circle is AIN SVP AVR or "Ain Soph Aur" and translates as "The Limitless Light." The energy of this circle corresponds to the life force that flows directly from God and infuses all existence.

If one were to imagine the diagram of the Great Egg as a three dimensional overhead view looking down a tube, then the concentric circles could be analogous to the Phi spiral of Sacred Geometry as it emanates downward from Infinite potential (AIN) toward each of us as individuals. If a diagram of The Tree of Life is then placed in the space within the center of the innermost circle, what results is an illustration of how each of us are connected to the eternal flow of energy between the Macrocosm and the Microcosm or "Above and Below" due to the fact that The Tree of Life is a prototype for the Human body. Aside from placing The Tree of Life into a larger theoretical context, this explanation of the Great Egg also provides the basis for the first connection I will make between The Tree and The Key of the Qabalistic Cross, namely that the top section of the Cross consists of the words "High" or "lofty" and "Light," a compilation of meanings that correspond quite nicely with the meaning of the innermost circle of The Great Egg, AIN SVP AVR or "The Limitless Light."

After the emanations of the Limitless Light have come forth from AIN SVP AVR, this energy then enters into the first sphere of each individual's Tree of Life to begin a zig-zag journey downward through the other 9 spheres. The name of the first sphere that receives these emanations is KThR or "Kether" meaning "Crown" which is the first word on the top line of the horizontal arm of "The Key of the Qabalistic Cross." The next word on the top horizontal line of the Cross is ABR, a notariqon corresponding to the initials of Ab, Ben, Ruach, or "Father, Son, and Spirit." The first aspect of this trinity, Ab (Father) would correspond to the second sphere on The Tree of Life known as "Chokmah" the Supernal Male Sphere which is analogous to the primordial Male energy or the great initiating force of the Universe. The third initial of the trinity is the letter R representing

Ruach or "Spirit" and this would correspond to the eternal potential represented by the third sphere on The Tree of Life known as "Binah" which signifies the Great Feminine archetype. The middle aspect of the trinity, Ben (the Son), would then be attributed to the sixth sphere on The Tree of Life known as "Tiphareth" an association I have derived from the traditional assignment of the V or "The Son" in IHVH being linked with the Heart Sphere of Tiphareth.

The second horizontal line of "The Key of the Qabalistic Cross" consists of the words ALH or "Goddess" and GBR or "Mighty Hero." Because of its literal meaning, ALH or "Goddess" can be said to correspond to the 2 feminine spheres within the Pillar of Mercy on The Tree of Life, Chesed, which represents how one embraces the world, and Netzach, the sphere of Artistic Creativity and Feminine Sexuality. From its literal meaning of "Mighty Hero" GBR can correspond to the 2 Male spheres on the opposing Pillar of Severity of the Tree, Geburah, which signifies how one seizes the world, and Hod, the sphere of the mental Body and Male Sexuality.

The only parts of The Tree of Life that remain to be fit into "The Key of the Qabalistic Cross" are the spheres of Yesod and Malkuth. Regarding the 9th sphere of Yesod, the great French Magi Eliphas Levi as well as the great Mystic Madame Blavatsky each associated the sphere with the Astral Plane or "The World of Dreams", that subtle realm which provides the foundation for our manifest physical reality. With this in mind, I believe that an analogy can be drawn between the sphere of Yesod and the final section or base of "The Key of the Qabalistic Cross" which contains the words AM (Mother), AI (Island), ISh (Essence), and ShM (The Name).

To begin this analogy let's pair the word AM with AI ("Mother" with "Island") and Ish with ShM ("Essence" with "The Name"). If "Mother" is taken to mean the higher, life giving properties which the Earth receives from the Sun," then an

"Island" would be a metaphorical moon that is reflective of the greater life-giving whole. Likewise, with the second pair of words, in that the "Essence" of something can only be partially reflected through language, or in this case, "The Name." This sort of subtlety represents the abstract yet essential qualities of what the Qabalah refers to as the "Foundation" of our earthly reality or "Yesod."

Now if the 4 letters at the base of The Cross can be shown to correspond to the characteristics of Yesod or "Foundation", then it should be possible if we follow the logic of the Qabalah that these characteristics would also in some way imply the essence of the earth sphere of Malkuth or "Kingdom" if Yesod was indeed the true "Foundation." In order to demonstrate this hypothesis, it will be necessary to regroup the four letters of this final section into a pair of three letter words that will overlap one another. The words formed will be, AMSh, which is a Qabalistic abbreviation for the three Mother elements of Air (A), Water (M), and Fire (Sh) and AISh or "Man." (An explanation of the Three Mother Elements was given earlier in this volume in Chapter III on Astrology).

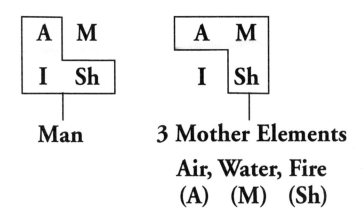

Illus. 74

If the meanings of these two words are then combined (Air + Water + Fire + Man) and Man were taken to represent the element of Earth as a result of both his habitation and dependency on the planet, then the four basic elements of material reality would be accounted for and thus an illustration of the sphere of Malkuth.

At this point, all 10 spheres of The Tree of Life can be recognized within "The Key of the Qabalistic Cross."

A R
R M   - Ain Soph Aur

Kether (Crown) - K Th R   A B R - Chokmah, Binah, Tiphareth

Chesed, Netzach - A L H   G B R - Geburah, Hod

A M
I Sh   - Yesod, Malkuth

Before moving on to an analysis of the Gematria, there is one more feature to be pointed out in the text of "The Key of the Qabalistic Cross." Within the pair of six letter lines that form the horizontal arms of the Cross, there are three smaller crosses expressed as a trio of X's created by the diagonal relationships between the vertical letters:

Illus. 75

The words formed by the three X's are;

KL	or	"All"
ATh	or	"You"
GR	or	"Proselyte"
HA	or	"Here"
BR	or	"Pure"
RB	or	"Rabbi"

From these words, I was able to derive the following description for The Tree of Life: "The **Pure Teacher** (Rabbi) that brings forth a new philosophy **(Proselyte)** for **You** to gain an understanding of the **All**."

In determining the Gematria for "The Key of the Qabalistic Cross," I have again divided the Key into the three sections that were used for the translation:

Section 1

A	R	(1 + 200)	=	201
R	M	(200 + 40)	=	<u>240</u>
		Total		441

A Hebrew word with the value of 441 is AMT or "Truth."

Section 2

K, Th, R, A, B, R (20 + 400 + 200 + 1 + 2 + 200) = 823
A, L, H, G, B. R (1 + 30 + 5 + 3 + 2 + 200)   = <u>241</u>

                                          Total 1064

1064 can be reduced to 1 + 0 + 6 + 4 or 11.
Some Hebrew words with values of 11 are AVD or "Light"
and ChG or "a circulatory form."

Section 3

A   M   (1 + 40)   =   41
I   Sh (10 + 300)   = <u>310</u>

            Total   351

Some Hebrew words with a value of 351 are AShIM or "The
Angels of Malkuth" and ANSh or "Man."

The total of the three sections (441 + 1064 + 351) is 1856
which can then be reduced to 1 + 8 + 5 + 6 or 20. Some other
words having a value of 20 are AChVH or "a Fraternity" and
ChZH or "A vision, a Prophet."

An interpretation for all the Gematria that has been stated so far would be:

A R R M	Ain Soph Aur (The Limitless Light)	or	Truth

K Th R A B R A L H G B R	Tree of Life Spheres 1 - 8	or	A circulatory form of Light (the Paths)

A M I Sh	Tree of Life Spheres 9 & 10	or	The Angels of Malkuth & Man, complementary aspects of reality.

Total	The complete Tree of Life & The Limitless Light	or	The Tree of Life as a vision of the Universe for the fraternity of Humanity.

Illus. 76

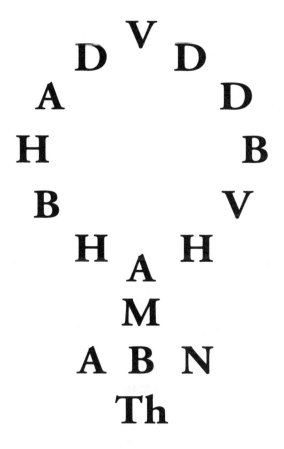

Illus. 77

Consisting of a circle that represents Spirit over a cross that represents matter, "The Key of Venus" is a reproduction of the Astrological symbol for the planet Venus, the celestial archetype symbolizing the highest vibration of the Goddess as it is expressed through the qualities of love, beauty, fruitfulness, and fecundity. For the translation of this Key, I will begin at the letter D (Daleth) that is situated the farthest to the right on the perimeter of the circle. Proceeding in a counter-clockwise direction, the first word formed is DD or "Love." As we continue to move counter-clockwise, the first word that was formed overlaps with the next word in that the last letter in DD becomes the first letter in DVD, the Hebrew name "David" which also translates literally as "Love." From this, one can see that the famous "Star of David" (or the hexagram) is actually a Star of Love expressing the union of "As Above, So Below" or the marriage of the heavens and the earth. Continuing along in the same direction around the circle, the next word formed is AHBH, which is yet another way of saying "Love" in Hebrew. The last word that is formed as we come around to complete the circle is AHVB or "Beloved."

Now that the circle has been translated, let's move next to the cross below it. The top letter of the vertical portion of the cross is A (Aleph) which is also part of the perimeter of the circle. By combining this "A" with the letter M or "Mem" directly under it, the resulting word is AM or "Mother." The next letter under "M" is B (Beth), and if this "B" is combined with the letter "Th" immediately below it, the word BTh or "Daughter" is formed.

The horizontal section of the cross consists of the letters A, B, and N which can be combined together to spell the word ABN or "Stone." It was mentioned earlier in the chapter on the Qabalah that for the Qabalistic Initiate the Hebrew word "Stone" is symbolic of "The Philosopher's Stone" of Alchemy in that the word is a coalescence of the two words, AB or "Father" and BN or "Son" which together would represent the essence of God the Father unified with that of His Earthly Son, or the Supreme consciousness and its earthly manifestation.

At this point, the reader should be aware that the cross in "The Key of Venus" contains the combined energies of the Father (AB) the Mother (AM) the Son (BN) and the Daughter (BTh) which are the very energies that constitute the Magickal Formula of Creation or "Tetragrammaton" (IHVH). These four energies in turn revolve around the central letter of the cross, B or "Beth," which translates as "a House" thus providing a symbolic earthly grounding for these basic archetypal energies.

Looking back at the circular portion of this Key, if we begin with the letter "A" that serves as the top letter of the cross and proceed in a clock-wise direction so as to isolate the letters situated at the four cardinal points on the perimeter, another cross will be formed by the letters A, H, V, and B which were seen earlier to form the word AHVB or "Beloved." The ubiquitous nature of "Love" is now reflected both above and below with the energy of IHVH in the cross connecting with the cross of AHVB within the circle. In addition, if lines were to be drawn to connect each opposing letter in the circular section of "The Key of Venus" 12 equal sections would be formed that would correlate with the 12 Houses of the Astrological Chart, thus reinforcing that the circle is a representation of Spirit (or the heavens) and the cross containing the energy of IHVH is the earthly manifestation of this Divine Spirit.

To compute the Gematria for "The Key of Venus," I first took the total of the 12 letters included in the circular portion of the Key:

$$D + D + V + D + A + H + B + H + A + H + V + B$$
$$4 + 4 + 6 + 4 + 1 + 5 + 2 + 5 + 1 + 5 + 6 + 2 = 45$$

Some other Hebrew words having the value of 45 are GAVLH, meaning "redemption" or "liberation" and ADM or "Man." The word ADM also contains within it a coalescence of meanings in that A or "Aleph" is a Qabalistic notation for both the element of Air and the One Infinite Creator, while DM is the Hebrew word for "Blood." Therefore the word ADM or "Man" can be explained as the result of the One Infinite Creator blowing the breath of life into the blood of humanity.

Next I computed the totals of the six letters that comprise the cross of "The Key of Venus."

A + M + B + Th + A + N
1 + 40 + 2 + 400 + 1 + 50 = 494 or 49 + 4

49 = 7 X 7 or the dimensions of the Magick Square of Venus (see Appendix II). Also 4 + 9 = 13 or the value of AHBH (Love).

4 = The 4 energies in IHVH, the 4 elements, the 4 directions, in short, the Natural World.

Total value of letters in the circle   45
and the letters in the cross   494
                           Total 539

539 can be reduced to 53 + 9 = 62 = the Hebrew word ASA or "Healing"

Thus from the Gematria of "The Key of Venus" it is revealed that through the Magick of Venus, which is expressed through "Love," we may gain redemption, liberation, and healing so as to transcend the limits of earthly existence and experience our Divine essence.

❖❖❖

Chapter X

Talismans

N this chapter I will present a series of my own original talismans after the style of the Sacred Seals exhibited in "The Key of Solomon the King," one of the two ancient manuscripts that were analyzed in chapter 8. Where my original Acrostic Keys were the result of Ritual Work and hence essentially philosophical in nature, the talismans that are included in this chapter are for the most part the result of Psychic Readings done with clients and were therefore designed to be healing tools in direct response to specific issues that arose during the sessions.

In the cases where a talisman was constructed from the data obtained during a counseling session, the clients input and ideas were always seriously considered in my subsequent planning of the design. The reason for this is because I feel it is absolutely necessary to include elements of the client's free will in the process so that any changes in their energy field which might come about because of the effect of the talisman will ultimately be consistent with their actual intentions for transformation and not what I interpret those intentions to be. I have also tried to be as direct as possible in describing the strategies behind the talismans as well as their subsequent effects, although I should point out that Healing on the Psychic level and then attempting to write about it are two diametrically opposed activities incorporating radically different sensibilities. Psychic Healing work is essentially a right brain activity which is intuitive and Neptunian in nature, while writing about the experience is a function of the left brain which is linear and Mercurial in nature. The bottom line is that I have tried to do my best in what amounts to describing the taste of an orange in terms of an apple.

TWO FOR "X"

I have chosen to title this section "Two for X" simply because the pair of talismans which will be discussed were both made for the same client, a woman I will hereafter refer to as "X."

The first talisman that I made for "X" (Illus. 78) was the result of a session in which I employed the use of The Tarot as well as channeled clairaudient and clairvoyant information. An important consideration expressed by the Client during this meeting was that she felt frustrated in her ability to manifest her Higher Creative energies. I sensed this as well and suggested that it would be to her advantage to try and tap into the higher energies of the Goddess within herself. An attractive and sought after woman, "X" was initially surprised by my statement. I then pointed out that while her life over the last fifteen years had been both adventurous and independent, it had also been primarily lived through the form of her inner warrior as a reaction to subconsciously sensing that her father had really wanted a son. Her amazement at my insight eventually helped her to realize that what she needed to be her most creative self would only come through embracing the vulnerability and sensitivity of her feminine or intuitive side, something which she had inadvertently repressed so as not to disappoint her father.

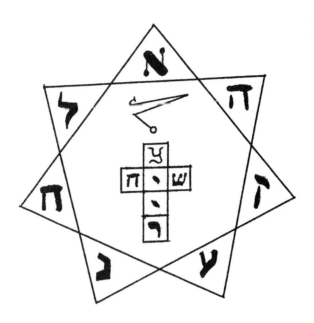

Illus. 78

In a conscious attempt to explore the different levels of the Goddess energy, I began by choosing the 7 pointed star of Venus or "The Heptagram" as the palette upon which to construct this talisman.

Reading the three upper points of the star in the order of top, upper left, then upper right, the Hebrew word illustrated in hieroglyphic letters is ALH or "Goddess" a coalescence that reveals within its spelling A, the One, and AL, a name for God the Father. Thus within the Hebrew word for Goddess we can see revealed the Supernal Triad of duality leading to Unity.

Going from top to bottom, the two lower points on the left side of the star contain the letters Cheth (Ch) and Nun (N) which together spell the word ChN or "Grace." This word is also a

Notariqon (acronym) for the term Chokmah Neserath or "The Secret Wisdom."

From top to bottom, the two lower points on the right side of the star contain the letters Ayin (O) and Zayin (Z) which together spell the word OZ or "Strength."

If the words formed by the letters in the seven points of the star are then combined together, they can be read as "The Grace (implying a "Secret Wisdom") and Strength of the Goddess.

At the top of the heptagon that constitutes the center of the star is a sigil of the client's name constructed from the Magick Square of Venus, while below that is a replica of the Rose Cross. Within the four squares that form the vertical portion of the Cross are the Hebrew letters Tzaddi (Tz), Yod (I), Yod (I), and Resh, which spell the word TzIIR or "Artist." The three horizontal squares of the cross contain the letters (from left to right) Cheth (Ch), Yod (I), and Shin (Sh). These three letters form two separate words, each word sharing the letter Yod in the central square. The first of these words is ChI or "Living" and the second is Ish or "Essence." All of the words contained in the cross can then be combined together to express "The living essence of the artist" or the creative sensibility emanating from the higher Self represented by the archetype of The Rose Cross.

My intention with this talisman was to evoke the dormant energies within the Sephirah of Netzach in "X's" Tree of Life, the sphere located on the left hip that is ruled by Venus and governs female sexuality as well as intuition and creative ability. "X" began sleeping with this talisman under her pillow the day I presented it to her, and within a short period of time reported to me that she had been having vivid dreams of her father in which she felt very angry and had to resist his sexual advances. In addition, she also found herself experiencing periodic soreness in her left hip although she had not been to the gym recently and had not strained herself in any way that she could remember. She was confused by the sexual aggressiveness toward her on the part of her father in these dreams, but then I explained to her that she was reexperiencing his subconscious rejection of her feminine identity when she was a girl. The talisman was stimulating her to see that it was only her father and not the world that rejected her femininity, hence there was no longer any reason for "X" to suppress the sensitivity that would allow her to be more creative in her life and work.

As a result of the success of the first talisman, "X" requested that I make her another one to enhance her lucid dreaming so that she might explore the Astral Plane more thoroughly (Illus. 79).

The World of Dreams or "The Astral Plane" is a place few are accomplished enough to deal with appropriately. The indoctrination imposed upon our conscious mind through education and societal pressure makes us think that the world of dreams is either a cryptic variation on conventional reality that any Psychiatrist can unravel to make sense, or that it's all just some weird entertainment not to be taken seriously, like "The X-Files." In actuality, the Dreamtime is an absolutely viable reality and occurrences there do impact on our lives, though often in ways conventional logic does not leave us equipped to understand. It is precisely for this reason that the overwhelming number of alien abductions occur during the Dream State when the victims are asleep and therefore unable to determine if what is happening to them is real or not. I have worked with individuals who have claimed to be abductee's and the pain and trauma that they describe from these experiences has left very real results. Some years ago, I was very nearly abducted although I was able to resist the experience because I had the presence of Spirit to be able to consciously focus on my Astral Body and project my free will against my attackers who were banking on me thinking the entire scenario wasn't real.

With the foregoing considerations in mind, I was very careful about how I constructed the second talisman "X" requested because I do not think the Occult realm or its tools are anything to be fooled with. As a Magician and Healer, I am bound by Universal Law to honor and respect an individual's free will, yet I also have a responsibility for my client's welfare once they have put their trust in me. With this second consideration in mind, I made a talisman for "X" which would only stimulate her to go as far into the Astral reality as her Higher Self deemed appropriate.

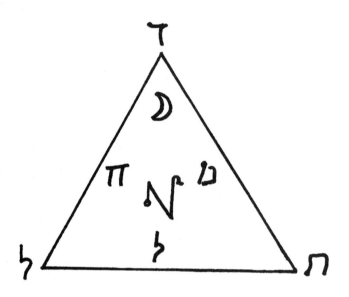

Illus. 79

The palette of Sacred Shape I chose was that of an equilateral triangle pointing upwards, the same form exhibited on the front of the robe worn by the Angel in the Tarot Card of Temperance XIV, the trump signifying balance as the way to achieve one's Higher Genius.

The Hebrew letters situated outside the perimeter of the triangle at the three angles should be read in the order of apex, lower left, lower right, so that the word DLTh or "Daleth" is formed, the literal spelling of the fourth letter of the Hebrew alphabet which translates as "a door."

The letters within the triangle should be read in the order of upper left, bottom, then upper right, so that the word ChLM or "dream" is formed. The planetary symbol within the triangle is that of the Moon, and the Sigil below it is of the client's name and was constructed from the Magick Square of the Moon.

The overall intention behind this talisman is to provide "a door" to "the dream" or the Astral Plane. The letters that form each of the words in this talisman are arranged so that they create a triangle pointing upwards and a triangle pointing downwards to mirror the interlaced equilateral triangles of the hexagram which expresses "As Above, So Below" or the reconciliation of "X's" conscious intentions with that of her Higher Will. The symbol of the Moon and the Sigil of the client's full name are then designed to forge a conscious connection with the Highest aspect of the Lunar archetype that exists within "X's" being.

As she had done with the first talisman, "X" slept with this one under her pillow and after a couple of days telephoned me to discuss the dreams that she had experienced. She was initially disappointed at not having traveled to one of the more exotic locations on the Astral Plane, but after some discussion did agree that these more recent dreams had made matters extremely clear regarding the issues of her father and her creativity that were brought up by the first talisman.

At this point, the reader has probably noticed that the results of the second talisman seem to be no more than a continuation of the work done by the first, which is essentially correct and serves to illustrate an important matter about Healing. The necessary thing to realize is that in any situation your Higher Self is always running the show, even though that might not seem to be the case based on surface appearances. What "X" wanted and what she really needed were two different things. Her Higher Self thought it was more important to address the issues with her Father rather than go "Astral Tripping" so that's exactly what happened. My concern for her safety, while part of my job, ended up being irrelevant (which I intuitively sensed), yet I took the proper precautions anyway because that's what I was meant to do. The meaning here is that ultimately we all heal ourselves through the act of living. The role of any Healer or Teacher is merely that of a facilitator who will assist by providing whatever information or guidance that our imbalances have caused us to overlook. The second talisman I made for "X" amounted to nothing much more than the service provided by a road sign on the highway, the difference in this case being that neither of us knew where she needed to go until she arrived there.

ONE FOR "Y"

The talisman in this section was created in response to what seemed to be a fairly straightforward problem of the everyday world, although when one does what I do for a living it becomes apparent after repeated experience that relatively little in the everyday world is without some underlying Spiritual ramification. In this case, a woman who is a friend and who I will refer to as, "Y" was having a great deal of difficulty organizing herself in her new apartment. Being someone who ordinarily possesses a thorough and industrious nature, "Y's" inability to get going in her living space seemed to me to be more about the space representing an aspect of her unfolding Higher Self rather than it merely being a physical place to get clean and livable. Initially she agreed with my diagnosis, though when I presented her with my idea for a talisman she had some trouble with the logic of it. In response to her skepticism, I made the point that what makes a great Artist is not merely the ability to allow their creative energy to flow, but more importantly that the energy being put forth can be channeled to manifest its highest potential within certain boundaries. For example, a great photograph is one that utilizes the limitations of the camera format so that the restrictions serve to showcase the unique vision of the Photographer. With this in mind, I subsequently chose the regular form of a square as the palette for this talisman in order to both direct and challenge "Y's" expansiveness, which I intended to stimulate with the planetary energy of Jupiter (Illus. 80).

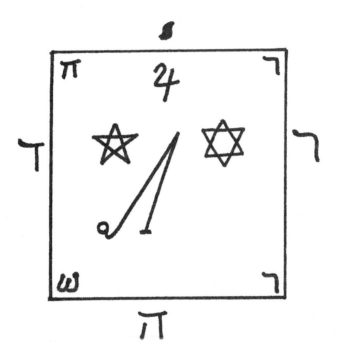

Illus. 80

Beginning on the left side of the square and proceeding clockwise, the four letters outside the perimeter are D (Daleth), I (Yod), R (Resh), and H (Heh), which together form the word DIRH or "Apartment." Using the inner angle of the square situated on the lower left as a starting point and again proceeding clockwise, the letters within the perimeter are Sh (Shin), Ch (Cheth), R (Resh), and R (Resh), which together spell the word

ShChRR or "to set free, liberate, or release." In addition to the Hebrew words, the talisman also contains the symbol for the planet Jupiter (located within the square just below the top side) and underneath that a Sigil of the client's name derived from the Magick Square of Jupiter. On either side of the Sigil are symbols for both the five and six pointed star that signify respectively the beginning and completion of "The Great Work."

From the preceding information, a summary of this talisman would be, "Within the boundaries of her apartment (symbolized by the labeled square), "Y" will be stimulated to expand (the archetype of Jupiter) in order to attain the alignment and unification of her living space. This expansion will in turn be a direct reflection of a deeper inner liberation that will represent a more conscious connection with her Higher Self (symbolized by the Pentagram and Hexagram)."

The strategy behind this talisman then was to redirect the Spiritual energy that is the true force behind the material world, when mundane circumstances seem to be an insurmountable obstacle to gaining a conscious connection with One's Higher Self.

ONE FOR "ME"

The next talisman I will write about is one that I constructed for my own personal use. Last summer I was contacted by a former colleague who asked if I would be interested in working as a Psychic Reader at a corporate picnic. Although it was made clear to me that I was being approached as an entertainer, I didn't look at the venue in that light, instead I firmly believe that whenever my gift is solicited, it is always for the reasons of Higher Healing and enlightenment despite what the solicitor's intentions may be. After agreeing to take the assignment, I subsequently received a phone call from the production coordinator to brief me on what was planned and how I would be expected to perform. It turned out that seven Psychics had been booked to read for what was expected to be a crowd of approximately 2000 people. I couldn't help but laugh. The thought of seven of us doing readings for 2000 people during the course of an afternoon was utterly ridiculous. After expressing my skepticism, I was then assured by this person on the phone that only about 200 of the people attending would actually want readings. Rather than setting my mind at ease, this news only made me acutely aware of the sort of situation I would be dealing with. It was just as absurd for seven of us to read for 200 people in an afternoon as it would be to read for 2000 or 2 million! Nonetheless, I knew that I was meant to do this and that there would be people there who needed to hear what I would have to say. My intuition was telling me that I would deal with as many individuals as Spirit wanted me to and that would be the end of the matter.

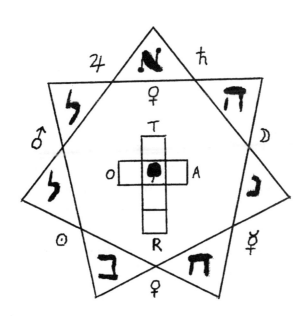

Illus. 81

As the day of the event drew closer I began to feel that some sort of Magickal intervention was going to be necessary, however, the way things appeared, it seemed as if nothing short of the miracle described in the parable of "The Loaves and the Fishes" would make it possible for me to fulfill my obligation to the large group I would be dealing with. It was then that an idea struck me. I had been making talismans for both friends and clients for a while now and getting good results so why not make one for a mass gathering (Illus. 81).

The Sacred Shape I chose for my palette was the seven-pointed Star of Venus. One reason for this selection was because I figured reading for all those people would be comparable to "The Little Old Lady who lived in a shoe she had so many children she didn't know what to do" and the power of the Goddess would be the only way to go. A second reason was because Venus is the planetary energy that rules Occult practices, and my abilities as a Practitioner of the Sacred Arts was certainly going to be tested. The major reason though for my selection of a Sacred Shape so closely aligned with the energies of Venus was because on the day of the event the planetary sphere of Venus was going to be in the Sign of Cancer conjunct with my natal Moon in the 10th House. Involved in this aspect would be the planet ruling the Occult (Venus) joined with the planet ruling Intuition (The Moon) in the Sign ruled by the Moon (Cancer), with the entire scene being enacted in the House that governs Career and appearing before the public. Not only was this an excellent energy to attempt something as challenging as reading for so many people, I also felt that it was a very definite omen that I was destined for the task.

I will begin my analysis of this talisman by translating the various Hebrew letters within the points of the star. Reading the top three points in the order of apex, upper left, and upper right, the letters are A (Aleph), L (Lamed), and H (Heh) which together spell the word ALH or "Goddess." This word was also utilized in an earlier talisman where it was explained that it is a coalescence revealing duality (ALH and AL) leading to Unity (A).

The letters contained in the two points on the lower left reading from top to bottom are L (Lamed) and B (Beth) which spell the word LB or "Heart."

The letters in the pair of points on the lower right reading from top to bottom are Ch (Cheth) and N (Nun) which spell the word ChN or "Grace." This word was also used in an earlier talisman and aside from its literal meaning it is also a Notariqon (Acronym) for Chokmah Neserath or "The Secret Wisdom."

The final word formed within the star includes the letters in the two lowest points, and if these letters are read from right to left they spell the word ChB or "Bosom."

A synthesis of the words contained within the seven points of the star would then be "The Higher Energy of The Goddess bestows upon us her Heart and Grace (which reveals a Secret Wisdom) that nurtures us (to her Bosom)".

In each of the outer angles between the points of the star are the symbols for the seven planets known to the Ancients. Proceeding clockwise from the upper right they are Saturn, the Moon, Mercury, Venus, the Sun, Mars, and Jupiter. These are the traditional attributions of the planets to these angles and in this particular instance I intended them to support the concept of Venus as the common ray of Love that unites all the planetary energies.

Within the central Heptagon of the star, directly under the uppermost point, is the planetary symbol of Venus. It should be noted that this symbol is directly over the symbol of Venus located in the angle between the two lowest points of the star, thus signifying the unification of the energies of Venus from above with those from below. Also in the central heptagon is a reconstruction of the Rose Cross of six squares with the letters T A R and O at the four cardinal points. The symbolism of The Rose Cross was explained in the Chapter entitled "Sacred Shapes" while the letters spelling TARO were deconstructed in the Chapter entitled "The Tarot," specifically in the section covering the "Wheel of Fortune

X." The significance of my using these letters in this talisman was because I would be employing the cards of The Tarot as my major tool during the time I would be reading at the picnic.

I constructed this talisman the day before the event and then consecrated it the next morning before I left. The result of my efforts was that I was able to draw in enough energy to read for the entire afternoon with only a single break, that brief respite coming about only because one of the production assistants had noticed that I was the only reader who had not yet taken a break and they were concerned if I was okay. I had been so wrapped up within the energy of my work that I failed to notice that my bladder was about to explode, so upon being interrupted I excused myself and dashed to the bathroom. After that I became totally immersed in my readings so that I didn't even notice the event was over until I finished with what turned out to be my last client and discovered my colleagues had been all packed up and ready to leave for some time. The production coordinator then notified me that I had 3 minutes to eat my free lunch and then the transportation for the Psychics was leaving.

The next day, a friend of mine, who was also one of the readers, told me that the production people were very annoyed with me because I was taking too long with the readings. When I thought back over the clients I dealt with during the course of that afternoon, there had been a woman who was going to leave her husband of 20 years, another individual who had recently had a parent die, as well as a whole bunch of people who hated their job, or felt Spirits around them, or had experienced some sort of Psychic phenomenon and had no one to talk to about it. I was right in my assumption that there would be people there who needed Healing and not just entertainment, so when I defended going overtime on most all of my readings, my friend explained good naturedly "What really annoyed the producers was that the line of people waiting to see you was easily twice as long as the line to see anyone else".   ❖❖❖

CHAPTER XI

THE BIRTH TALISMAN

will begin this chapter by re-introducing something that was only partially explained in the section on Astrology when mention was made of how the 360 degree circle of the Astrological chart can be divided into 72 equal sections known as "Quinaries." Each of these sections encompass 5 degrees of the total circle and are attributed an Angelic name which collectively are known as "The Schemhamphorasch." The literal translation of this word from Hebrew is "The Divided Name" and it refers to the various manifestations of God through the forms of His Angelic servants. The Qabalistic formula for determining these variations of the Divine Essence is derived from Chapter 14 of Exodus, specifically verses 19, 20, and 21 which describe the cloud of dust and darkness brought upon the Egyptians by the Angel of the Elohim and how this darkness instead became light for the escaping Hebrews so they might see their way to the Red Sea ahead of their pursuers. The verses culminate with Moses using his Magickal powers to part the waters of the Red Sea, which subsequently collapse again upon the Egyptians once the Jews have safely passed. In Hebrew each of these three verses from Exodus contain 72 letters, which are then manipulated through permutation or "Temurah" to form 72 three-letter names. Each of these names are then attached a suffix of either "AL" signifying

severity and judgment or "IH" signifying mercy and beneficence. The 72 names are then divided into 4 groups of 18 with each of them corresponding to one of the letters in the Tetragrammaton (IHVH), hence the analogy of this collection of Angelic titles to the divided name of God.

What follows is a table of these names in their Hebrew spellings along with how they relate to the Astrological chart.

Sign	Degree	Days	Angelic Name	Planet Ruling Decan
Aries	0 - 4	3/20 - 3/24	HchShIH	Mars
	5 - 9	3/25 - 3/29	OMMIH	Sun
	10 - 14	3/30 - 4/03	NNAIL	Sun
	15 - 19	4/4 - 4/8	NIThAL	Venus
	20 - 24	4/9 - 4/13	MBHIH	Venus
	25 - 29	4/14 - 4/18	PVIAL	Mercury
Taurus	0 - 4	4/19 - 4/23	NMMIH	Mercury
	5 - 9	4/24 - 4/28	IILAL	Moon
	10 - 14	4/29 - 5/4	HRChAL	Moon
	15 - 19	5/5 - 5/9	MIRAL	Saturn
	20 - 24	5/10 - 5/14	VMBAL	Saturn
	25 - 29	5/15 - 5/19	IHHAL	Jupiter
Gemini	0 - 4	5/20 - 5/24	ONVAL	Jupiter
	5 - 9	5/25 - 5/30	MChIAL	Mars
	10 - 14	5/31 - 6/4	DMBIH	Mars
	15 - 19	6/5 - 6/9	MNQAL	Sun
	20 - 24	6/10 - 6/14	AIOAL	Sun
	25 - 29	6/15 - 6/20	ChBVIH	Venus

Sign	Degree	Days	Angelic Name	Planet Ruling Decan
Cancer	0 - 4	6/21 - 6/25	RAHAL	Venus
	5 - 9	6/26 - 6/30	IBMIH	Mercury
	10 - 14	7/1 - 7/5	HIIAL	Mercury
	15 - 19	7/6 - 7/11	MVMIH	Moon
	20 - 24	7/12 - 7/16	VHVIH	Moon
	25 - 29	7/17 - 7/21	ILIAL	Saturn
Leo	0 - 4	7/22 - 7/26	MITAL	Saturn
	5 - 9	7/27 - 7/31	OLMIH	Jupiter
	10 - 14	8/1 - 8/6	MHShIH	Jupiter
	15 - 19	8/7 - 8/11	LLHAL	Mars
	20 - 24	8/12 - 8/16	ANAIH	Mars
	25 - 29	8/17 - 8/21	KHThAL	Sun
Virgo	0 - 4	8/22 - 8/26	HZIAL	Sun
	5 - 9	8/27 - 9/1	ALDIH	Venus
	10 - 14	9/2 - 9/6	LAVIH	Venus
	15 - 19	9/7 - 9/11	HHIIH	Mercury
	20 - 24	9/12 - 9/16	IZLAL	Mercury
	25 - 29	9/17 - 9/22	MBHAL	Moon
Libra	0 - 4	9/23 - 9/27	HRIAL	Moon
	5 - 9	9/28 - 10/1	HQMIH	Saturn
	10 - 14	10/2 - 10/6	LAZIH	Saturn
	15 - 19	10/7 - 10/12	KLIAL	Jupiter
	20 - 24	10/13 - 10/17	LVVIH	Jupiter
	25 - 29	10/18 - 10/22	PHLIH	Mars
Scorpio	0 - 4	10/23 - 10/27	NLKAL	Mars
	5 - 9	10/28 - 11/1	IIIAL	Sun
	10 - 14	11/2 - 11/6	MLHAL	Sun
	15 - 19	11/7 - 11/11	HHVIH	Venus
	20 - 24	11/12 - 11/16	NThHIH	Venus
	25 - 29	11/17 - 11/21	HAAIH	Mercury

Sign	Degree	Days	Angelic Name	Planet Ruling Decan
Sagittarius	0 - 4	11/22 - 11/25	IRThAL	Mercury
	5 - 9	11/26 - 11/30	ShAHIH	Moon
	10 - 14	12/1 - 12/5	RIIAL	Moon
	15 - 19	12/6 - 12/10	AVMAL	Saturn
	20 - 24	12/11 - 12/15	LKBAL	Saturn
	25 - 29	12/16 - 12/20	VShRIH	Jupiter
Capricorn	0 - 4	12/21 - 12/25	IChVIH	Jupiter
	5 - 9	12/26 - 12/30	LHChIH	Mars
	10 - 14	12/31 - 1/4	KVQIH	Mars
	15 - 19	1/5 - 1/8	MNDAL	Sun
	20 - 24	1/9 - 1/13	ANIAL	Sun
	25 - 29	1/14 - 1/19	ChOMIH	Venus
Aquarius	0 - 4	1/20 - 1/23	RHOAL	Venus
	5 - 9	1/24 - 1/28	IIZAL	Mercury
	10 - 14	1/29 - 2/2	HHHAL	Mercury
	15 - 19	2/3 - 2/7	MVKAL	Moon
	20 - 24	2/8 - 2/12	VVLIH	Moon
	25 - 29	2/13 - 2/17	ILHIH	Saturn
Pisces	0 - 4	2/18 - 2/22	SALIH	Saturn
	5 - 9	2/23 - 2/27	ORIAL	Jupiter
	10 - 14	2/28 - 3/4	OShLIH	Jupiter
	15 - 19	3/5 - 3/9	MIHAL	Mars
	20 - 24	3/10 - 3/14	VHVAL	Mars
	25 - 29	3/15 - 3/19	DNIAL	Mars

THE SHEMHAMPHORASCH IN THE ZODIAC WHEEL

♈	♉	♊	♋	♌	♍
1-HchShIH	7-NMMIH	13-ONVAL	19-RAHAL	25-MITAL	31-HZIAL
2-OMMIH	8-IILAL	14-MChIAL	20-IBMIH	26-OLMIH	32-ALDIH
3-NNAIL	9-HRChAL	15-DMBIH	21-HIIAL	27-MHShIH	33-LAVIH
4-NIThAL	10-MIRAL	16-MNQAL	22-MVMIH	28-LLHAL	34-HHIIH
5-MBHIH	11-VMBAL	17-AIOAL	23-VHVIH	29-ANAIH	35-IZLAL
6-PVIAL	12-IHHAL	18-ChBVIH	24-ILIAL	30-KHThAL	36-MBHAL

Illus. 82

♎	♏	♐	♑	♒	♓
37-HRIAL	43-NLKAL	49-IRThAL	55-IChVIH	61-RHOAL	67-SALIH
38-HQMIH	44-IIIAL	50-ShAHIH	56-LHChIH	62-IIZAL	68-ORIAL
39-LAZIH	45-MLHAL	51-RIIAL	57-KVQIH	63-HHHAL	69-OShLIH
40-KLIAL	46-HHVIH	52-AVMAL	58-MNDAL	64-MVKAL	70-MIHAL
41-LVVIH	47-NThHIH	53-LKBAL	59-ANIAL	65-VVLIH	71-VHVAL
42-PHLIH	48-HAAIH	54-VShRIH	60-ChOMIH	66-ILHIH	72-DNIAL

To make a Birth Talisman, one must first locate their day of birth in the preceding chart along with the corresponding name of the Angel which rules that particular day. Aside from the 72

Quinaries, the Astrological chart can also be divided into 36 sections of 10 degrees known as "Decans" each having a ruling planet that is specified in the last column on the right in the previous chart. This is important because in order to make a Birth Talisman the name of the Angel attributed to that day must be transformed into a Sigil and the planet ruling the Decan will determine which Magick Square needs to be used. Although most of the Angelic names will seem unpronounceable to the English reader, this is only because the names are in their Hebrew spellings, which is absolutely necessary in order to be able to fashion a Sigil from any of the Magick Squares. The astute reader will also notice that from the top of the chart to the bottom, the planets ruling the Decans are in the recurring order of Mars, the Sun, Venus, Mercury, the Moon, Saturn, and Jupiter. Following is a diagram explaining the rationale behind this order.

Energy	♂
Light	☉
Love	♀
Translation	☿
Emotions	☽
Structure	♄
Expansiveness	♃

A summary of the diagram might be "The raw, Divine **Energy** transmitted as **Light** and **Love** can only be **Translated** in human terms as **Emotions** whose **Structure** must then be mastered in order to **Expand** back to the true source."

Once a Sigil of the Angelic name for a birthday has been made from the Magick Square of the planet ruling the corresponding Decan, this Sigil may be put into a palette of Sacred Shape along with any other symbols that may complement the overall intention behind the talisman. The choice of a Sacred Shape can be based on either the Magician's intuition or the energy associated with the planet governing the Decan associated with the Angel's name. What follows is a suggested list of how the

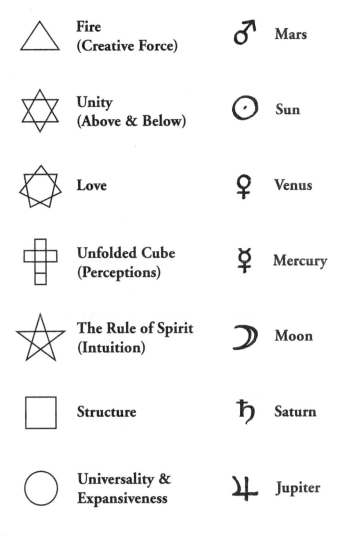

△ Fire (Creative Force)	♂ Mars
✡ Unity (Above & Below)	☉ Sun
Love	♀ Venus
Unfolded Cube (Perceptions)	☿ Mercury
☆ The Rule of Spirit (Intuition)	☽ Moon
☐ Structure	♄ Saturn
○ Universality & Expansiveness	♃ Jupiter

Illus. 8.3

various Sacred Shapes may be matched up with the planets.

To conclude this chapter, I will present a Birth Talisman that I made for myself so that the reader can get an idea of how to begin to make their own.

Name: Thomas

Name in Hebrew: ThmSh

Birthday: 9/28 or 5⁰ Libra

Angelic Name for 5⁰ Libra: HQMIH

Planet ruling Decan: Saturn

Sigil (reduced using Aiq Bkr and the Magic Square of Saturn)

Illus. 84

For my palette of Sacred Shape I chose the Star of Venus because it corresponds to the planet that rules my birth Sign (Libra). In the top three points of the star, I have included a Qabalistic spelling of my first name (ThMSh), while in the left and right points respectively are the symbols for the Astrological Sign of Libra (♎) and the planet Saturn (♄) (the planet ruling the Decan of my birthday). Each of the two bottom points contain the Hebrew letter Daleth (D) and the word they spell is DD or "Love." My choice of this word holds a special significance in that the numerical value of Daleth is 4, and by repeating it to spell "Love", my age at the time I made this talisman is revealed (44). The upper portion of the central heptagon within the star contains the symbol for the planet Venus and below that is the Sigil of the Angel ruling my birthday.

❖❖❖

PART V

A Manual Of Ritual

CHAPTER XII

SOME NOTES ON RITUAL

HE preceding chapters have provided a great deal of basic information in regard to creating a talisman, however, it should be kept in mind that these constructions intrinsically contain no more power than any other inanimate object. In order for a talisman to be effective, it must first be charged or "electrified" through Ritual. By engaging in this rite of empowerment, the reader will then be taking that first giant step beyond simply being an academic student of Magick and entering into the realm of actually pursuing The Great Work.

The practice of Ritual Magick has traditionally always had a strong theatrical element in its presentation. What I mean by this is that the various implements that are considered to be the necessary tools of the Magician have been chosen for their symbolic value, hence the more demonstratively these tools are used, the greater their effect is supposed to be. Theoretically I agree with this, yet history has revealed that Ritual for its own sake can quickly become dogma, which in turn is perhaps the greatest of all obstacles to true Spiritual Enlightenment. The most important aspect of Magick is not the robe, sword, or wand the operator may or may not have, but rather the integrity, focus, clarity, and intent which the practitioner brings to the performance of the ritual. When I first began doing Ritual Work, I used my index finger as a wand. As my technique developed I started to acquire some of the traditional paraphernalia associated with the Western Magickal Tradition, though over time I also began to incorporate some of my own original Magickal tools. The Art of Magick is about personal enlightenment and self-empowerment, and the natural by-products of such attainments are originality and creativity. The Magickal Tradition presented so far in this book has been that of Judeo-Christian Europe and to some extent Ancient Egypt, yet the fact is that Magickal Traditions have existed all throughout the world at various times. I firmly believe that all Spiritual Paths ultimately lead to the same place, therefore to my mind it is valid to borrow from any tradition as long as what is being used resonates in your heart and serves the purpose at hand.

Having just presented an opinion in favor of a more laissez-faire approach to Magickal Practice, I will now retrace my steps for a moment and add that I do believe there is one absolutely necessary element for sustained and effective Ritual Work, namely an altar.

When most people think of an altar, an image comes to mind of a Mass being performed in one of the great cathedrals of Europe complete with museum quality marble statues and a jewel encrusted gold chalice. Although I do feel an altar is the single necessary aspect of Ritual Work, I also have a pretty liberal definition of what constitutes an altar. In the most practical terms, an altar is merely a surface upon which the Magician will place his or her implements. Whether this surface is a table like the one used in the image of The Magician from the Tarot, or if it is a piece of decorated cloth laid on the ground like the "Mesas" of the indigenous Peruvian Shamans, all that is important is that the operator have a specific place where the metaphors of his intention can be organized to be effectively directed to their highest purpose. For example, my altar at the time of writing this book was a second-hand antique night-table which I covered with a large piece of dark velvet. I had additionally placed this setting for my Magickal efforts in the area of my apartment corresponding to

"Helpful Friends" in the Feng Shui bagua. The Oriental practice of Feng Shui is a very potent Magickal tool and I intuitively felt that my Ritual Work would be well served if it were consistently done in the area of my living space corresponding to the energies that are supportive of my Highest Being. It was my choice to use an actual piece of furniture for my altar, although someone else with perhaps a different set of considerations might opt for something more portable like the earlier mentioned "Mesas" of the Peruvian Shamans. In either case, all that is ultimately important is that a grounded environment be created for One's Higher Self to manifest and abide in.

There will be two formal rituals spoken of in this section "The Lesser Banishing Ritual of the Pentagram" and "The Ritual of the Hexagram." Of these two, the former is for consecration and the later is for empowerment. In this context, what is meant by consecration is both purification and protection, while empowerment implies the invocation of specific energies with certain effects in mind.

At this point, it is important to address that it is not always possible to know in advance what the full range of a Ritual Working will yield. For those who are more linear in their perceptions, this might seem to indicate that Ritual Work is far too vague to be trusted, although this seeming inexactness actually makes perfect sense because the human Magician is not yet as pure as the higher archetypal energies that he or she hopes to invoke. Thus a talisman consecrated to manifest one thing or another might initially only accentuate the blockages that exist within the Magician concerning the intended outcome. Since balance is the single irrefutable law of Magick, a reverse effect like the one previously described will not discourage the astute practitioner, rather he or she will recognize the setback as a healing crisis and understand that overcoming any obstacles that arise will act to establish a necessary foundation from which a greater good will eventually manifest.

Another important point to remember that was written about earlier is that the energies invoked by the Magician through Ritual Work are not necessarily outside powers, rather they are metaphors of the higher aspects of the self. Therefore, if the Magician wishes to invoke the planetary energy of Mars to aid his efforts in some conflict, in actuality he is really calling upon the archetype of Mars within him to rise up and manifest. For the experienced Magician, this psychoanalytical perspective does not represent merely a Modernist deconstruction of Magick, instead it expresses a true understanding of the direct connection between the individual self and a unified, universal consciousness. It should also be added that tracing the source of power back to the self does not make the subsequent effect of a Ritual any less impressive or real.

One last point that also needs to be made clear is that the text of the following rituals are aids for self-empowerment and transformation, not strategies to manipulate Spirits or Multidimensional energies for simple ego gratification. It is not necessary to employ Magick to create imbalance or illusion. Plain old everyday material reality already has quite sufficient means for that type of activity.

❖❖❖

CHAPTER XIII

THE LESSER BANISHING RITUAL OF THE PENTAGRAM

I N the chapter on "The Qabalah" an operation was discussed known as "Squaring the Circle" where it was shown that the five-pointed star or "Pentagram" represents Spirit presiding over the material world. Another way of explaining this would be to look at the Pentagram as a representation of the human figure with the uppermost point corresponding to the head and the four lower points corresponding to the arms and legs.

Illus. 85

Just as the head containing the brain governs the processes of the body and the relationship of that body to the world at large, so should the higher faculties of Spirit govern the material existence of a human being.

According to the renowned French Magician Eliphas Levi (1810 - 1875), "The Pentagram expresses the mind's domination over the elements and it is by this sign that we bind the demons of air, the spirits of fire, the specters of water, and the ghosts of earth. It is the Star of the Magi, the burning Star of the Gnostic Schools, the sign of intellectual omnipotence and autocracy." For the Qabalistic Magician, the Pentagram represents the beginning of The Great Work in that it represents the reaching of the human form toward its Higher Genius. The elemental Spirits that Levi speaks of in his definition are the raw energies of being (mind, creative fire, emotions, and physical being) that we each must come to master in order to embody the Higher Awareness aspired to through the form of the Pentagram.

As a result of their association to the material world, the four lower points of the Pentagram are each assigned one of the four basic elements in Western Occultism.

Illus. 86

The Lesser Banishing Ritual of the Pentagram can be used for any of the following purposes (1) Protection (2) to clear one's energy field or rebalance the energy in a given space (3) to purify and consecrate an area in preparation for Magickal or Healing Work. The Ritual of the Pentagram is also excellent as a daily Spiritual routine, so that the stress of modern living does not knock one too far out of a balanced awareness of the Higher Self (the top point of the Pentagram).

The ceremony itself consists of two basic techniques (1) making the Qabalistic Cross and (2) tracing the Pentagram (Five-pointed Star).

THE QABALISTIC CROSS

To make the Qabalistic Cross, begin by touching your forehead with your right hand and saying "ATOH" (Thou Art).

With the same right hand touch your breast and say "MALKUTH" (the Kingdom)

Touch your right shoulder and say "VE-GEBURAH" (of the Power)

Touch your left shoulder and say "VE-GEDULAH" (and the Glory)

Finish by bringing your hands together in prayer position over your breast and saying "LE-OLAM (Forever) AMEN.

MAKING THE PENTAGRAM
(Five-pointed Star)

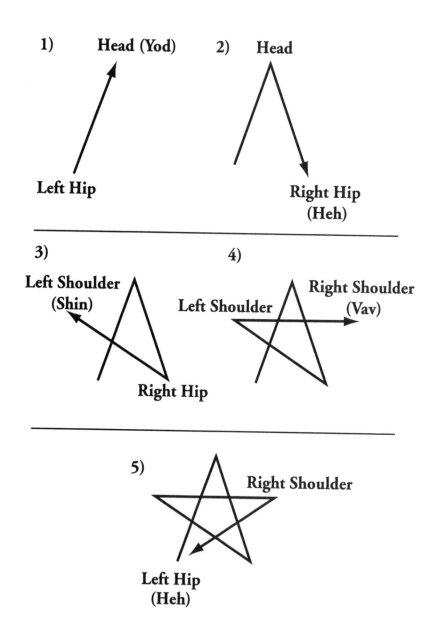

To trace the Five-pointed Star, begin by taking your right hand with the index finger extended and placing it on your left hip. Next, with one strong, continuous movement, trace the Star in front of you as per the instructions in Illustration 87 while at the same time voicing the Hebrew letters in parenthesis when you get to each of the five points of the Star. The letters designated in the following illustration form the name YHShVH (Jeheshuah) or "Jesus" and symbolize Spirit (the letter Shin) descended into the formula for earthly creation (IHVH).

THE RITUAL

When the making of the Qabalistic Cross and the tracing of the Star have been committed to memory, then one is ready to perform the complete ritual.

1 - Begin by facing east and making the sign of The Qabalistic Cross.

2 - Remain facing east and trace the Star while voicing the designated Hebrew letters. After that, extend your arm and point into the center of the Star while toning the letters "Yod Heh Vav Heh" (IHVH).

3 - Turn next to the south, trace the star once again while voicing the designated letters, then point to the center of the star and tone the name "Adonai" (Aah-do-noy) which translates as "Lord."

4 - Turn now to the west, trace the star while saying the letters, and then tone "AHIH" (Eh-heh-yeh) which means "Existence."

5 - Turn finally to the north, trace the star and say the letters one last time, and then tone "AGLA" (Ogla), an acronym for "Atoh Gebor Le-Olam Adonai or "Thou Art Mighty Forever, O Lord!"

6 - Face the east once again and recite the following;

"Before me I summon the Archangel Raphael
Behind me I summon the Archangel Gabriel
To my right I summon the Archangel Michael
To my left I summon the Archangel Auriel
Before me flames the Pentagram (trace a five-pointed star)
Behind me shines the Six-rayed Star (trace a 6 pointed Star)"

7 - At this point the operator should express in their own words the reason for the Ritual (protection, consecration, etc.) as well as any thoughts or feelings that seem appropriate.

8 - To complete the Ritual close the circle by repeating the Qabalistic Cross.

An important aspect to keep in mind when performing any ritual is that I would encourage the practice of what Aleister Crowley termed "Enflaming one's self with prayer" whereby a conscious emotional connection is established with the object of one's Spiritual devotions. An example of this concept in everyday life would be when one speaks intimately with a lover in the coital embrace. At no time should the Ritual of the Pentagram (or any ritual) ever be performed in a mechanical fashion just as lovemaking should never be performed perfunctorily.

❖❖❖

CHAPTER XIV

THE RITUAL
OF THE HEXAGRAM

ONSISTING of two interlocking equilateral triangles with their apexes pointing in opposite directions, the six-pointed star or "Hexagram" represents the union of the heavens and earth. Where the Pentagram represented the human figure and expressed the mastery of mind infused with Spirit over the material world, the Hexagram signifies "As Above, So Below" and represents the descent and subsequent unification of Spirit with material form. It would only seem fitting then that the Pentagram should be used for protection, consecration, and purification, while the Hexagram is utilized for invocation and union. In considering the Hexagram as a vehicle for Magickal work, let us first look at how the Qabalists used the symbol in relation to their knowledge of Ancient Cosmology. Illustration 88 is a diagram applying the seven planets known in Antiquity to the six-pointed star.

In order to better facilitate further discussion on the significance of the way the planets are applied to the Hexagram, I will present a brief review of the planetary archetypes that were discussed in the chapter on "Astrology."

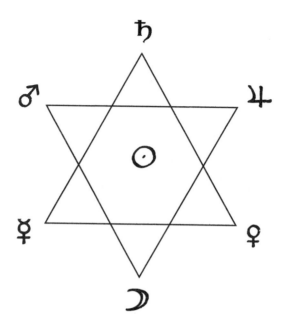

Illus. 88

Often referred to as "The Teacher" Saturn (♄) is the archetype of structure and directly relates to our life lessons in terms of the obstacles and limitations we must deal with.

Jupiter (♃) is the archetype of expansiveness, generosity, growth, and optimism.

The highest vibration of the Goddess, Venus (♀) is the archetype of beauty, love, and fruitfulness, as well as the ray through which all the other planets must be filtered because love is the basic energy of the Universe.

The Moon (☽) represents the subconscious and the emotions within us. She is the shadowy sister of Venus and her energy governs the Astral Plane.

Mercury (☿) represents the mental faculties and communication. The God Mercury invented both Magick and

Tarot as ways to codify the realm of Psychic phenomenon.

Mars (σ) signifies raw force and is the archetype of war, conflict, strength, and ultimately ego.

The Sun ($\odot$) represents the light of Higher Consciousness and is placed in the center of the hexagram to signify the connection of Earthly Man to the Higher Genius.

The planets of Neptune, Uranus, and Pluto were unknown to the Ancients and therefore not included in the diagram. The subsequent association of these planets to the points of the Hexagram is based on their affinities to the energies of the other established archetypes.

Neptune (Ψ) would be a higher, more ethereal and diffuse vibration that could be associated with Mercury, with the former representing the Psychic knowledge codified by the later in the Tarot.

Uranus ($\uranus$) is a freer, more radical and less structured energy also associated with Mercury.

Pluto ($\pluto$) is a more transformative and Spiritual vibration of Mars.

When connecting the preceding information to Ritual Work, the Hexagram then becomes a conduit for the unification of the higher archetypal energies of the planets with the reflections of those same energies within each individual human being.

The basis of Qabalistic Magick is balance that is clearly expressed through the polarities illustrated in the various spheres that constitute the diagram of The Tree of Life. This concept of balance is also evident in the way the Hexagram is used as a

Magickal tool, for in the act of Ritual Invocation the two interlocking triangles of the six-pointed star need to be drawn from an awareness of opposing energies. During a ritual, the tracing of the first triangle must commence from the point on the star that represents the energy to be invoked, while the second triangle needs to be started from the point directly opposite from where the first triangle began. For example, to invoke the archetype of Venus, the initial triangle would be drawn in the air in front of one starting from the point on the Hexagram attributed to Venus. The drawing of the second triangle that would complete the Hexagram would then be started from the point attributed to Mars that lies directly opposite the position of Venus. As a result of this approach, the opposing energies are utilized to stimulate one another to manifestation, much in the same way that the sexual tension between male and female creates new life on the physical plane.

With this understanding of the dynamics of the Hexagram as a Magickal tool, let us now explore the actual Ritual of the Hexagram.

First it needs to be determined what planetary energy the operator wishes to invoke. Illustration 89 is a chart of the planetary symbols, Hebrew call word, God Names, and in some cases Hebrew letters particular to each planet.

The word "ARARITA" that serves as a call word for each planetary Hexagram is a Notariqon (Acronym) for the Hebrew sentence, "One is his beginning, One is his individuality, his permutation is One" (see Chapter II page 34). The inclusion of this word and the sentence it implies should be looked upon as an additional reinforcement of the previously stated concept that by invoking a planetary energy, one is in effect merely calling forth the aspects of that archetype which already exist within. A further expression of this concept would be to also realize "One is my beginning, one is my individuality, my permutation is one."

Planet	Symbol	Call word, God Name, Hebrew letter

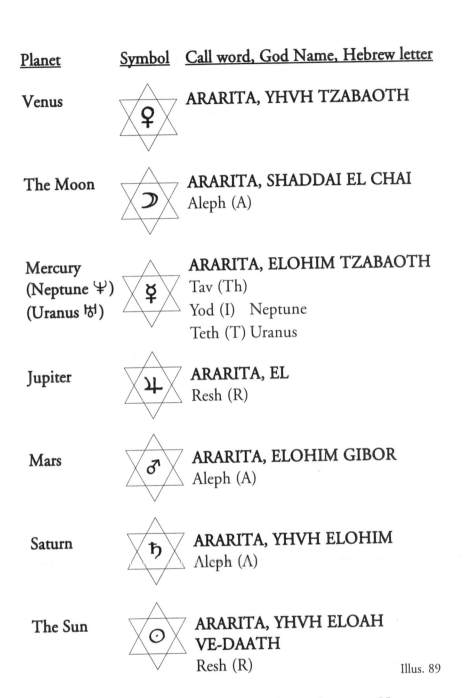

Venus — ARARITA, YHVH TZABAOTH

The Moon — ARARITA, SHADDAI EL CHAI
Aleph (A)

Mercury
(Neptune ♆) — ARARITA, ELOHIM TZABAOTH
(Uranus ♅) Tav (Th)
Yod (I)   Neptune
Teth (T) Uranus

Jupiter — ARARITA, EL
Resh (R)

Mars — ARARITA, ELOHIM GIBOR
Aleph (A)

Saturn — ARARITA, YHVH ELOHIM
Aleph (A)

The Sun — ARARITA, YHVH ELOAH
VE-DAATH
Resh (R)

Illus. 89

*To invoke the energy of the Sun, all six planetary Hexagrams need to be drawn in order beginning with Saturn and proceeding clock-wise around the points of the star (see Illus. 88).

THE RITUAL

The actual Ritual of the Hexagram consists of five sections (1) making the Qabalistic Cross (2) drawing the hexagrams for the 4 directions (3) performing the operation of LVX/ INRI/ IAO (4) tracing the Grand Hexagram of Invocation (5) moving the planetary energy invoked through one's Tree of Life.

1) Begin by facing east and making the Qabalistic Cross (See the instructions for this in the chapter on The Lesser Banishing Ritual of the Pentagram).

2) Drawing the Hexagrams for the 4 directions involves a different procedure for each direction. Using your right hand with the index finger extended, trace the triangles that compose the Hexagram as per the following instructions, making sure to begin at the point representing the planetary energy you wish to invoke.

*When drawing the pair of triangles, the solid one in the following diagrams is to be drawn first. After drawing the triangle in each direction, follow it up by voicing the call word, God Name, and Hebrew letter for the planet invoked. In the following diagrams Venus is being used as an example.

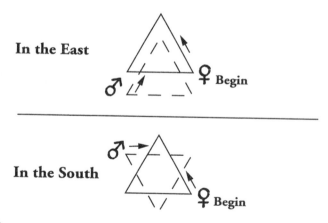

Illus. 90

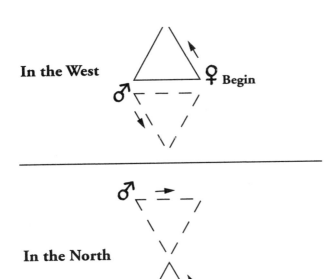

In the West

In the North

Illus. 90

3) After tracing the final Hexagram in the north, complete the circle by turning back to where you began in the east. While facing east, execute the ensuing postures and recite the accompanying formula for LVX.

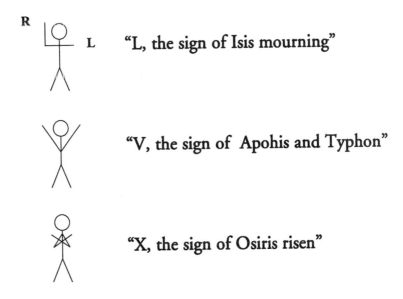

"L, the sign of Isis mourning"

"V, the sign of Apohis and Typhon"

"X, the sign of Osiris risen"

Illus.91

Repeat the positions again, but this time say;

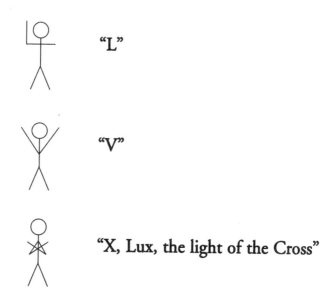

"L"

"V"

"X, Lux, the light of the Cross"

Illus. 92

Next, assume the position of Christ on the Cross and recite the following formula for INRI/IAO.

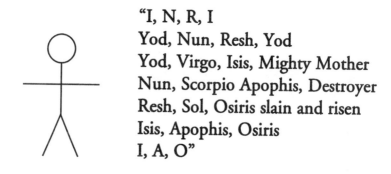

"I, N, R, I
Yod, Nun, Resh, Yod
Yod, Virgo, Isis, Mighty Mother
Nun, Scorpio Apophis, Destroyer
Resh, Sol, Osiris slain and risen
Isis, Apophis, Osiris
I, A, O"

Illus. 93

"INRI" is the Latin inscription, "Jesus of Nazareth, King of the Jews," that was hung on the cross over Christ's head when he was murdered. This inscription is then literally translated into Hebrew and what follows are the esoteric associations to each letter.

I = Yod, the Hebrew letter attributed to the 20th Pathway on The Tree of Life. The Astrological association is Virgo, the Virgin, who was Mary to the Christians and Isis to the Egyptians.

N = Nun, the Hebrew letter attributed to the 24th Pathway on The Tree of Life. The Astrological association is Scorpio, the sign of death and transformation, which in the formula is expressed as "Apophis" the great evil serpent in Egyptian Mythology.

R = Resh, the Hebrew letter attributed to the 30th Pathway on The Tree of Life. The Tarot Card associated with this Path is The Sun XIX which in the Waite / Smith deck depicts the conquering Child Horus astride a white horse. This child is supposed to represent the resurrected form of his father Osiris who was slain by the evil serpent Apophis.

The first letter of the names Isis, Apophis, and Osiris can then be combined together to form a Notariqon (Acronym) that forms the Greek word IAO which is the Gnostic name for the One Infinite Creator.

4) After acting out and reciting the formula for LVX / INRI / IAO, relax from the position of the cross and allow your arms to hang loosely at your sides. With your right hand now draw a large Hexagram in the air before you making sure to begin at the point of the star that corresponds to the planetary energy you wish to invoke. In the center of this star draw the symbol for the planet in question. This is the Grand Hexagram of Invocation. After

drawing this star, follow it up by voicing the call word, God Name, and Hebrew letter.

At this point, a vortex has now been created to receive the higher energies of the planet that has been summoned. While doing this Ritual, it is important to keep in mind that by summoning the higher energy of a planet one is really only activating that same archetypal energy lying dormant within the self. Keep in mind as well that your physical body during the Ritual represents a metaphorical Hexagram uniting above and below. From this moment on in the ceremony, the words must be your own. Be aware that as you speak to the Planet / God being invoked, you are a representation of that Planet / God. This role transference is extremely important in that it is a device to activate the Higher Self through direct identification with a God form. The purpose of the Ritual leading up to this moment of spontaneous dialogue was to set a stage upon which the individual can now hear directly from their Higher Self.

5) After having said whatever you felt was necessary, the last portion of the ritual consists of moving the planetary energy which has just been invoked through the 10 Spheres of your Tree of Life. Illustration 94 is a diagram of The Tree of Life applied to the human body along with the path you should visualize the energy moving along.

This route through the Sephiroth is known as "The Path of the Flaming Sword." Begin to direct the energy you have summoned by first imagining your Crown Sphere (Kether #1) opening like a Lotus to receive the energy of the planet in question. After you have visualized this energy moving downward through all 10 Spheres in numerical order, it will then be necessary to say aloud "Kether is in Malkuth (the 10th sphere of the Tree of Life located at the feet)." Next visualize the energy moving upward along the same path. Upon the arrival of this energy back into the sphere of

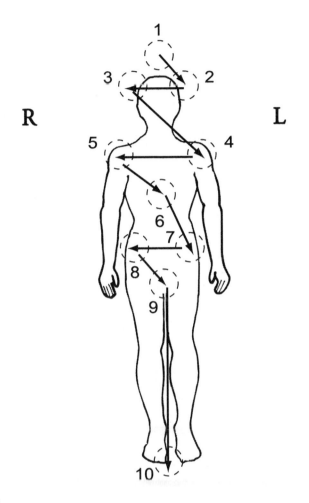

R   L

Illus. 94

Kether, it will then be necessary to say "Malkuth is in Kether" thereby reinforcing the essential "As Above, So Below" aspect of the Hexagram. While imagining the energy traveling first downward and then upward along The Path of the Flaming Sword, it helps me if I tone for one full breath between each sphere. The regulation of my breathing as well as the sound created by the tone aids me in focusing my concentration so that I can lose myself and become completely "enflamed with prayer." Of course this is just my personal preference and I would encourage each individual to discover on their own what feels right for them. When you have completed this last part of the Ritual and can feel the energy of whatever planet you have called upon filling your body, you may then engage in another period of improvised dialogue or simply bask in the power you have summoned. To close the Ritual, perform "The Qabalistic Cross" while facing east.

Although The Lesser Banishing Ritual of the Pentagram and The Ritual of the Hexagram have been presented separately, they can be performed together. If one is simply seeking protection or cleansing some negative energy then the Ritual of the Pentagram can be performed by itself. However, if one wishes to invoke a planetary energy, then The Ritual of the Pentagram should precede the Hexagram Ritual so that the work area will be consecrated and purified for the subsequent vortex of Six-pointed Stars. If a talisman is to be charged, then The Ritual of the Hexagram should not be closed until the Magician has performed the technique in the next chapter to electrify the talisman.

❖❖❖

CHAPTER XV

THE SIGN OF
THE ENTERER OF THE
THRESHOLD
& THE SIGN OF SILENCE

NCE the working space has been consecrated with The Ritual of the Pentagram and a vortex has been established to invoke higher energies through The Ritual of the Hexagram, another set of steps are necessary if one wishes to consecrate and empower a talisman. These steps are added onto The Ritual of Hexagram and are called respectively, "The Sign of the Enterer of the Threshold (The Sign of the E.T)" and "The Sign of Silence."

Symbolic of reaching forward in search of the truth, the Sign of the E.T represents the channeling of a Higher Light through the Magician into the material world. Because this is a technique for focusing and projecting "The Magickal Will" the Sign of the E.T is considered a symbol of great attacking force hence its usefulness as a method through which to charge a talisman.

To perform The Sign of the E.T, one needs to begin by facing the altar (or wherever the talisman to be charged is resting) while maintaining a relaxed posture with the arms hanging loosely at one's sides. Because the desired planetary energy has already been invoked through The Hexagram Ritual, the operator should be imagining that he or she is standing within a ring of Hexagrams that are radiating this energy through their body.

THE SIGN OF THE E.T.

1 - Initial position
(side view)

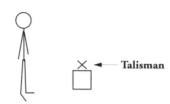

2 - Step and raise arms

3 - Complete the step and
thrust arms forward

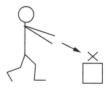

Illus.95

Begin by raising the left foot and then advancing it approximately 12 inches while at the same time raising both arms above the head as though reaching to receive the light from above. As the advancing step is completed, the arms should be lowered to eye level so that the hands are extended forward with the palms facing down. The operator's back should now be slightly arched as their arms are extended straight ahead with the fingertips pointing directly at the talisman. With conscious effort, the Magician needs to imagine next that all the power of the planet that was invoked is streaming out from both his eyes and fingertips toward the talisman infusing it with the highest and purest energy.

The final position for The Sign of the E.T should be maintained until the Magician feels that the talisman has been adequately charged. In performing this technique, I like to take a deep breath and tone while my attention is fixed on the talisman, repeating my inhaling and toning as many times as the number for the planet being invoked. For example, I would emit three tones for Saturn, four tones for Jupiter, five tones for Mars, etc..

Once the talisman has been fully charged, the flow of energy must then be discontinued or else the operator will become weakened. To stop the flow of Astral Energy the Magician needs to perform "The Sign of Silence" (Illus. 96).

To begin, drop your arms to your sides and bring the left foot back to its original position so that the heels of both feet are together. Next, stamp down once with the left foot while raising your left arm and placing the index finger on the center of your lips. While in this position imagine a protective concentration of Astral Light enveloping your body like a thick mist. Aside from being useful in discontinuing the flow of energy started by The Sign of the E.T, The Sign of Silence also provides a means for protection and can be used as a quick form of Psychic Defense if one hasn't the time to perform a Pentagram Ritual.

Once the charging of the talisman is completed, the Magician can then make any closing comments he or she may deem appropriate before eventually closing the entire operation with a performance of "The Qabalistic Cross."

❖❖❖

THE SIGN OF SILENCE

1 - Lower arms and
  withdraw original step

2 - Stamp left foot and
  raise left arm

3 - Complete foot stamp
  and touch lower lip
  with left index finger

Illus.96

APPENDICES

SACRED SHAPES
(FORMS FOR TRACING)

THIS Appendix includes line drawings suitable for tracing of each of the 7 Sacred Shapes discussed in Chapter 6.

CIRCLE

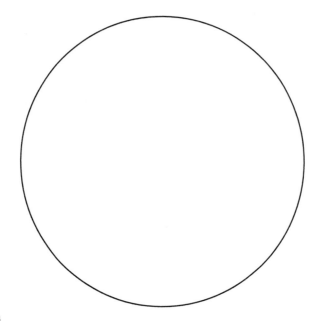

Illus. 97a

TRIANGLE

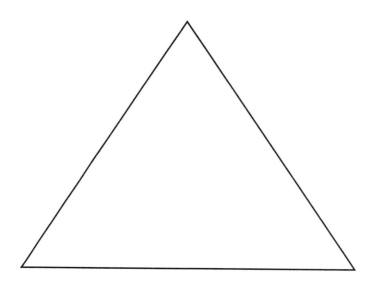

Illus. 97b

SQUARE

Illus. 97c

PENTAGRAM

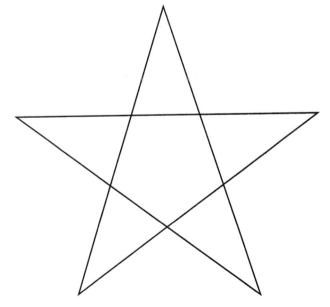

Illus. 97d

HEXAGRAM

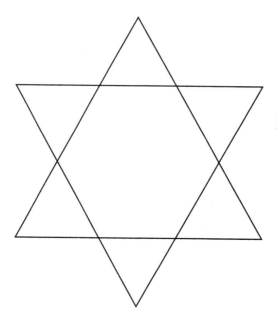

Illus. 97e

HEPTAGRAM (Broad Points)

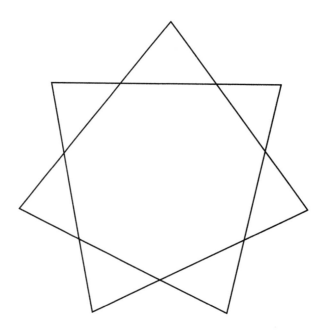

Illus. 97f

HEPTAGRAM (Sharp Points)

Illus. 97g

ROSE CROSS

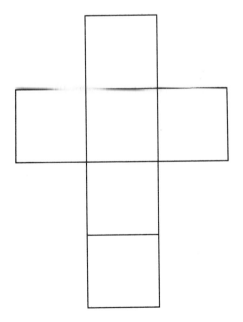

Illus. 97h

MAGICK SQUARES

OR those who wish to further explore the construction of Sigils, this section includes the Magick Squares of the seven planets along with their corresponding Angelic Names, Intelligences, and Spirits in both Hebrew and English. It should be noted that the Angelic Beings and Intelligences associated with each planet were thought to be benevolent energies, while the Spirits were considered to be darker and of a negative nature. I have also included the Mystic Numbers for each planet as they are derived from their respective Magick Squares, which include; A) the number of the planet itself; B) the number of squares within each grid; C) the total of each line in the square; and D) the grand total of each square.

SATURN

4	9	2
3	5	7
8	1	6

Illus. 98

Angel: **Cassiel (KShIAL)**
Intelligence: **Agial (AGIAL)**
Spirit: **Zazel (ZAZL)**

Mystic Numbers
A) **3**
B) **9**
C) **15**
D) **45**

JUPITER

4	14	15	1
9	7	6	12
5	11	10	8
16	2	3	13

Illus. 99

Angel: **Sachiel (SChIAL)**
Intelligence: **Iophiel (IHPIAL)**
Spirit: **Hismael (HSMAL)**

Mystic Numbers
A) **4**
B) **16**
C) **34**
D) **136**

MARS

11	24	7	20	3
4	12	25	8	16
17	5	13	21	9
10	18	1	14	22
23	6	19	2	15

Illus. 100

		Mystic Numbers	
Angel:	Zamael (ZAMAL)		A) 5
Intelligence:	Graphiel (GRAPIAL)		B) 25
Spirit:	Bartzabel (BRTzBAL)		C) 65
			D) 325

THE SUN

6	32	3	34	35	1
7	11	27	28	8	30
19	14	16	15	23	24
18	20	22	21	17	13
25	29	10	9	26	12
36	5	33	4	2	31

Illus. 101

		Mystic Numbers	
Angel:	Michael (MIKAL)		A) 6
Intelligence:	Nakhiel (NKIAL)		B) 36
Spirit:	Sorath (SVRTh)		C) 111
			D) 666

VENUS

22	47	16	41	10	35	4
5	23	48	17	42	11	29
30	6	24	49	18	36	12
13	31	7	25	43	19	37
38	14	32	1	26	44	20
21	39	8	33	2	27	45
46	15	40	9	34	3	28

Illus. 102

Angel: **Hanael (HANAL)**
Intelligence: **Hagiel (HGIAL)**
Spirit: **Kedemel (QDMAL)**

Mystic Numbers
A) **7**
B) **49**
C) **175**
D) **1225**

MERCURY

8	58	59	5	4	62	63	1
49	15	14	52	53	11	10	56
41	23	22	44	45	19	18	48
32	34	35	29	28	38	39	25
40	26	27	37	36	30	31	33
17	47	46	20	21	43	42	24
9	55	54	12	13	51	50	16
64	2	3	61	60	6	7	57

Illus. 103

Angel: **Raphael (RPAL)**
Intelligence: **Tirial (TIRIAL)**
Spirit: **Taphthartharath (ThPThRThRTh)**

Mystic Numbers
A) **8**
B) **64**
C) **260**
D) **2080**

THE MOON

37	78	29	70	21	62	13	54	5
6	38	79	30	71	22	63	14	46
47	7	39	80	31	72	23	55	15
16	48	8	40	81	32	64	24	56
57	17	49	9	41	73	33	65	25
26	58	18	50	1	42	74	34	66
67	27	59	10	51	2	43	75	35
36	68	19	60	11	52	3	44	76
77	28	69	20	61	12	53	4	45

Illus. 104

		Mystic Numbers
Angel:	Gabriel (GBRIAL)	A) 9
Intelligence:	Malkah be Tarshisim ve-ad	B) 81
	Ruachoth Schechalim	C) 369
	(MLKA BThRShISIM VOD	D) 3321
	RVChVTh ShChLAM)	
Spirit:	Schad Barschamoth ha-Shartathan	
	(ShD BRShMOTH HShRThThV)	

GLOSSARY OF SOME USEFUL HEBREW WORDS

HIS section consists of a brief list of Hebrew words in Romanized letters along with the English translations. I have purposely limited this section to small words containing 2, 3, or 4 letters in order to facilitate the needs of the beginning student as he or she attempts to express their intentions within the limited confines of the various Sacred Shapes. Also included are the Hebrew names for the Basic and Alchemical elements, Earthly Kingdoms, and the Planets.

General Words

AA - Abbreviation of ARIK ANPIN or "The Vast Countenance" (the Macrocosm)

AB - Father

ABA - Father

AD - Mist

AV - Desire

AVB - the dark fire of Lower Magick

AVD - the Divine Fire of Higher Magick

AVR - the Light of day

AT - Enchantment

AL - God

AM - Mother

AMA - the unfertilized Mother

ASA - Healing

AR - Light

AShP - Magician

ATh - Essence

BA - to come and go

BB - Vein

BL - Lord

BN - Son

BR - Pure

BTh - Daughter

ChG - a Feast

ChVL - the Phoenix

ChI - Living

ChN - Grace (also a Notariqon for Chokmah Neserath or "Secret Wisdom"

DB - A Bear

DD - Love

DVD - David or Love

DIN - Justice

DM - Blood

DOTh - Daath or "Knowledge"

DTz - Rejoice

DTh - The Law

GL - Spring or Fountain

GLA - to Reveal

GN - Garden

GP - Self

HD - Echo

HR - Mountain

IM - Sea

ITzA - Emerge

ISh - Being

KCh - Power

KL - All

KS - Throne

KP - Palm of the hand and a Notariqon for the Greek, Kties Phallos or "The Vagina and the Phallus," otherwise the Sacred Union of Tantra

LA - Not

LB - Heart

MQ - Decay

MSh - Silk

MTh - Dead

NM - Slumber

NS - Miracle

NR - Candle

ON - God

OZ - Strength

PN - Face

PZ - Gold

QTz - End

RB - Rabbi (Teacher)

RVCh - Air, Spirit, Wind, Mind

RK - Compassion

RM - High, lofty

SVS - Horse

SM - Poison

SLCh - Forgive

ShM - The Name

ShSh - Marble

TITh - Serpent

ThV - A Cross

ThM - Perfect

ThN - A Dragon

ThO - Time

TzGB - Lust

TzLB - Cross

TzM - People

TzQRB - Scorpion

VRD - Rose

ZA - Abbreviation for Zauir Anpin or "The Lesser Countenance" (the Microcosm)

ZK - Purity

ZRCh - to rise as the Sun to give light

The Four Elements

ASh - Fire

MIM - Water

RVCh - Air

HARTz - Earth

Alchemical Elements

GVPRITh - Sulphur

MLCh - Salt

KSPITh - Mercury (Quicksilver)

Earthly Kingdoms

MINRLI - Mineral

IRQ - Vegetable

BHMH - Animal

ANRShI - Human (also ADM - Man)

Planets

ShBThAI or "Shabbathai" - Saturn

TzDQ or "Tzedeq" - Jupiter

MADIM or "Madim" - Mars

ShMSh or "Shemesh" - The Sun

NVGH or "Nogah" - Radiance or Venus

KVKB or "Kokav" - A Star or Mercury

LBNH or "Levannah" - White or The Moon

BIBLIOGRAPHY

BIBLIOGRAPHY

Case, Paul Foster, **The True and Invisible Rosicrucian Order**
(Samuel Weiser 1985)

Crowley, Aleister, **Book 4**
(Samuel Weiser 1980)
777 and Other Qabalistic Writings
(Samuel Weiser 1973)
The Book of the Law
(Samuel Weiser 1976)
Magick in Theory and Practice
(Castle 1991)

Levi, Eliphas, **Transcendental Magic**
(Samuel Weiser 1970)

Mathers, Samuel Liddell,
The Key of Solomon the King
(Samuel Weiser 2000)
The Book of the Sacred Magic of Abramelin the Mage
(Dover 1975)
The Kabbalah Unveiled
(Routledge & Kegan Paul LTD.. 1962)

Regardie, Israel, **A Garden of Pomegranates**
(Llewellyn 1970)
The Golden Dawn
(Llewellyn 1989)

Sivan, Reuven & Levenston, Edward A.,
**The New Bantam-Megiddo Hebrew
& English Dictionary**
(Bantam 1975)

Waite, Arthur Edward,
The Pictorial Key to the Tarot
(University Books 1959)

NOTES

NOTES

NOTES

NOTES